Scientific Autobiography and Other Papers

by

MAX PLANCK

With a Memorial Address on Max Planck,
by MAX VON LAUE

Translated from German
by

FRANK GAYNOR

PHILOSOPHICAL LIBRARY
New York

ISBN 0-8065-3075-8

PRINTED IN THE UNITED STATES OF AMERICA

Scientific Autobiography
and Other Papers

Max Planck

Contents

Titles of Essays as they appeared in the German original:

Wissenschaftliche Selbstbiographie (1948)

Scheinprobleme der Wissenschaft (1947)

Sinn und Grenzen der Exakten Wissenschaft (1947)

Religion und Naturwissenschaft (1947)

Der Kausalbegriff in der Physik (1948)

Introduction

delivered by Max von Laue
in the Albani Church in Göttingen
on October 7, 1947

My Fellow Mourners:

We stand at the bier of a man who lived to be almost four-score-and-ten. Ninety years are a long life, and these particular ninety years were extraordinarily rich in experiences. Max Planck would remember, even in his old age, the sight of Prussian and Austrian troops marching into his native town of Kiel. The birth and meteoric ascent of the German Empire occurred during his lifetime, and so did its total eclipse and ghastly disaster. These events had a most profound effect on Planck in his person, too. His eldest son, Karl, died in action at Verdun in 1916. In the Second World War, his house went up in flames during an air raid. His library, collected throughout a whole long lifetime, disappeared, no one knows where, and the most terrible blow of all fell when his second son, Erwin, lost his life in the rule of terror in January, 1945. While on a lecture tour, Max Planck, himself, was an eye-witness of the destruction of Kassel, and was buried in an air raid shelter for several hours. In the middle of May, 1945, the Americans sent a car to his estate of Rogätz on the Elbe, then a theatre of war, to take him to Göttingen. Now we are taking him to his final resting-place.

In the field of science, too, Planck's lifetime was an epoch of deep-reaching changes. The physical science of our days shows an aspect totally different from that of 1875, when Planck began to devote himself to it—and Max Planck is entitled to the lion's share in the credit for these changes. And what a wondrous story his life was! Just think—A boy of seventeen, just graduated from high school, he decided to take up a science which even its most authoritative representative whom he could consult, described as one of mighty meager prospects. As a student, he chose a certain branch of this science, for which even its neighbor sciences had but little regard—and even within this particular branch a highly specialized field, in which literally nobody at all had any interest whatever. His first scientific papers were not read even by Helmholtz, Kirchhoff and Clausius, the very men who would have found it easiest to appreciate them. Yet, he continued on his way, obeying an inner call, until he came face to face with a problem which many others before him had tried and failed to solve, a problem for which the very path taken by him turned out to have been the best preparation. Thus, he was able to recognize and to formulate, from measurements of radiations, the law which bears and immortalizes his name for all times. He announced it before the Berlin Physical Society on October 19, 1900. To be sure, the theoretical substantiation of it made it necessary for him to reconsider his views and to fall back on methods of the atom theory, which he had been wont to regard with certain doubts, And beyond that, he had to venture a hypothesis, the audacity of which was not clear at first, to its full extent, to anybody, not even to him. But on ·December 14, 1900, again before the German Physical Society, he was able to present the theoretic deduction of the law of radiation. This was the birthday of the quantum theory. This achievement will perpetuate his name forever.

This is why on this day innumerable scientific bodies have expressed their sympathy and grief over his death, in telegrams, or by sending their representatives here. Thus, we have with us now the President of the Academy of Berlin, and the Rector of the University of Berlin, two bodies with which Max Planck was especially closely affiliated. He taught at the University for more than forty years, and he was a member of the Academy for more than half a century; in fact, most of that time he held the office of one of its four Permanent Secretaries. Likewise, the Academies of Munich and Göttingen are represented here by their Presidents, the University of Göttingen by its Rector, and the School of Engineering of Hannover by its Faculty delegate. Furthermore, wreaths have been placed on the bier in behalf of the State Government of Lower Saxony.

I would like to mention, in particular, some of the many wreaths lying here. One of them was sent by the German Museum in Munich, which is just about to place Max Planck's bust in its Hall of Fame. Next to the respects paid by the Academy of Munich, this wreath is the last salute from Bavaria, where Planck grew up, and where he would spend his vacation every year, to seek and find pleasure and relaxation.

Another wreath is inscribed: "The German Physical Societies to their Honorary Member." These Societies remember the fifty-eight years of Planck's membership, his selfless work in the most diverse administrative posts; for the major part of his membership he was a member of the Board, and also held its chairmanship several times. They remember, in particular, the great many enlightening lectures which he delivered at their scientific meetings, and above all, that address in 1900 when, as mentioned before, he made his first disclosure of his law of radiation and its deduction. A bright ray of his brilliant fame was thus reflected on the German Physical Society, too.

And here is a plainer wreath, without any streamers. It was placed here by me in behalf of all his pupils, among whom I count myself, as a perishable token of our never-ending affection and gratitude.

A Scientific Autobiography

My original decision to devote myself to science was a direct result of the discovery which has never ceased to fill me with enthusiasm since my early youth—the comprehension of the far from obvious fact that the laws of human reasoning coincide with the laws governing the sequences of the impressions we receive from the world about us; that, therefore, pure reasoning can enable man to gain an insight into the mechanism of the latter. In this connection, it is of paramount importance that the outside world is something independent from man, something absolute, and the quest for the laws which apply to this absolute appeared to me as the most sublime scientific pursuit in life.

These views were bolstered and furthered by the excellent instruction which I received, through many years, in the *Maximilian-Gymnasium* in Munich from my mathematics teacher, Hermann Müller, a middle-aged man with a keen mind and a great sense of humor, a past master at the art of making his pupils visualize and understand the meaning of the laws of physics.

My mind absorbed avidly, like a revelation, the first law I knew to possess absolute, universal validity, independently from all human agency: The principle of the conservation of energy. I shall never forget the graphic story Müller told us, at his *raconteur's* best, of the bricklayer lifting with great effort a heavy block of stone to the roof of a house. The work he thus performs does not get lost; it remains stored up, perhaps for many years, undiminished and latent in the block of stone, until one day the block is perhaps loosened and drops on the head of some passerby.

After my graduation from the *Maximilian-Gymnasium,* I attended the University, first in Munich for three years, then in Berlin for another year. I studied experimental physics and mathematics; there were no professorships or classes in theoretical physics as yet. In Munich, I attended the classes of the physicist Ph. von Jolly, and of the mathematicians Ludwig Seidel and Gustav Bauer. I learned a great deal from these three professors, and I still retain them in reverent memory. But I did not realize until I came to Berlin that in matters concerned with science they had really just a local significance, and it was in Berlin that my scientific horizon widened considerably under the guidance of Hermann von Helmholtz and Gustav Kirchhoff, whose pupils had every opportunity to follow their pioneering activities, known and watched all over the world. I must confess that the lectures of these men netted me no perceptible gain. It was obvious that Helmholtz never prepared his lectures properly. He spoke haltingly, and would interrupt his discourse to look for the necessary data in his small note book; moreover, he repeatedly made mistakes in his calculations at the blackboard, and we had the unmistakable impression that the class bored him at least as much as it did us. Eventually, his classes became more and more deserted, and finally they were attended by only three students; I was one of the three, and my friend, the subsequent astronomer Rudolf Lehmann-Filhés, was another.

Kirchhoff was the very opposite. He would always deliver a carefully prepared lecture, with every phrase well balanced and in its proper place. Not a word too few, not one too many. But it would sound like a memorized text, dry and monotonous. We would admire him, but not what he was saying.

Under such circumstances, my only way to quench my thirst for advanced scientific knowledge was to do my own reading on subjects which interested me; of course, these were the subjects relating to the energy principle. One day, I happened to come across the treatises of Rudolf Clausius, whose lucid style and enlightening clarity of reasoning made an enormous impression on me, and I became deeply absorbed in his articles, with an ever increasing enthusiasm. I appreciated especially his exact formulation of the two Laws of Thermodynamics, and the sharp distinction which he was the first to establish between them. Up to that time, as a consequence of the theory that heat is a substance, the universally accepted view had been that the passing of heat from a higher to a lower temperature was analogous to the sinking of a weight from a higher to a lower position, and it was not easy to overcome this mistaken opinion.

Clausius deduced his proof of the Second Law

of Thermodynamics from the hypothesis that *"heat will not pass spontaneously from a colder to a hotter body."* But this hypothesis must be supplemented by a clarifying explanation. For it is meant to express not only that heat will not pass directly from a colder into a warmer body, but also that it is impossible to transmit, by any means, heat from a colder into a hotter body without there remaining in nature some change to serve as compensation.

In my endeavor to clarify this point as fully as possible, I discovered a way to express this hypothesis in a form which I considered to be simpler and more convenient, namely: *"The process of heat conduction cannot be completely reversed by any means."* This expresses the same idea as the wording of Clausius, but without requiring an additional clarifying explanation. A process which in no manner can be completely reversed I called a *"natural"* one. The term for it in universal use today, is: *"Irreversible."*

Yet, it seems impossible to eradicate an error which arises out of an all too narrow interpretation of Clausius' law, an error against which I have fought untiringly all my life. To this very day, instead of the definition I just mentioned, one often finds irreversibility defined as "An irreversible process is one which cannot take place in the opposite direction." This formulation is insufficient. For it is quite possible to conceive of a process which cannot take place in the opposite direction but which can in some fashion be completely reversed.

Since the question whether a process is reversible or irreversible depends solely on the nature of the initial state and of the terminal state of the process, but not on the manner in which the process develops, in the case of an irreversible process the terminal state is in a certain sense more important than the initial state—as if, so to speak, Nature "preferred" it to the latter. I saw a measure of this "preference" in Clausius' entropy; and I found the meaning of the Second Law of Thermodynamics in the principle that in every natural process the sum of the entropies of all bodies involved in the process increases. I worked out these ideas in my doctoral dissertation at the University of Munich, which I completed in 1879.

The effect of my dissertation on the physicists

of those days was nil. None of my professors at
the University had any understanding for its contents, as I learned for a fact in my conversations
with them. They doubtless permitted it to pass as
a doctoral dissertation only because they knew me
by my other activities in the physical laboratory
and in the mathematical seminar. But I found
no interest, let alone approval, even among the
very physicists who were closely concerned with
the topic. Helmholtz probably did not even read
my paper at all. Kirchhoff expressly disapproved
of its contents, with the comment that the concept
of entropy, whose magnitude could be measured
by a reversible process only, and therefore was
definable, must not be applied to irreversible
processes. I did not succeed in reaching Clausius.
He did not answer my letters, and I did not find
him at home when I tried to see him in person in
Bonn. I carried on a correspondence with Carl
Neumann, of Leipzig, but it remained totally
fruitless.

However, deeply impressed as I was with the
importance of my self-imposed task, such experiences could not deter me from continuing my
studies of entropy, which I regarded as next to

energy the most important property of physical systems. Since its maximum value indicates a state of equilibrium, all the laws of physical and chemical equilibrium follow from a knowledge of entropy. I worked this out in detail during the following years, in a number of different researches. First, in investigations on the changes in physical state, presented in my probationary paper at Munich in 1880, and later in studies on gas mixtures. All my investigations yielded fruitful results. Unfortunately, however, as I was to learn only subsequently, the very same theorems had been obtained before me, in fact partly in an even more universal form, by the great American theoretical physicist Josiah Willard Gibbs, so that in this particular field no recognition was to be mine.

While an instructor in Munich, I waited for years in vain for an appointment to a professorship. Of course, my prospects for getting one were slight, for theoretical physics had not as yet come to be recognized as a special discipline. All the more compellingly grew in me the desire to win, somehow, a reputation in the field of science.

Guided by this desire, I decided to submit a paper for the prize to be awarded in 1887 by the Philosophical Faculty of Göttingen. The subject to be discussed was, "The Nature of Energy." After I had completed my paper, in the spring of 1885, I was offered the associate professorship in theoretical physics at the University of Kiel. This offer came as a message of deliverance. The moment when I paid my respects to Ministerial Director Althoff in his suite in the Hotel Marienbad, and he informed me of the particulars and conditions of my appointment, was, and will always be, one of the happiest of my life. For even though my life in my parents' house was as beautiful and contented as any man could wish for, my longing for independence kept growing within me, and I was yearning for a home of my own.

To be sure, I suspected, and by no means without reason, that this smile of good fortune was actually not so much a reward for my scientific accomplishments as a practical result of the circumstance that Gustav Karsten, Professor of Physics in Kiel, happened to be a close friend of my father. Nevertheless, this realization could not

mar my supreme happiness, and I was firmly resolved to justify the confidence in me in every way
in my power.

I soon moved to Kiel, where I put the finishing
touches on my paper, and submitted it in Göttingen. It won second prize. Besides my entry, two
other papers had been submitted on the subject,
but these two were awarded no prize at all. Obviously, I was wondering why my paper had failed
to win first prize, and I found the answer in the
text of the detailed decision of the Faculty of
Göttingen. The judges set forth a few points of
criticism of minor import, and then stated:
"Finally, the Faculty must withhold its approval
from the remarks in which the author tries to
appraise Weber's Law." Now, the story behind
these remarks was: W. Weber was the Professor
of Physics in Göttingen, between whom and
Helmholtz there existed at the time a vigorous
scientific controversy, in which I had expressly
sided with the latter. I think that I make no mis-
take in considering this circumstance to have
been the main reason for the decision of the
Faculty of Göttingen to withhold the first prize
from me. But while with my attitude I had in-

curred the displeasure of the scholars of Göttingen, it gained me the benevolent attention of those of Berlin, the results of which I was soon to feel.

No sooner had I finished my paper for Göttingen than I returned to my favorite subject, and wrote a number of monographs, which I published under the collective title, *On The Principle of the Increase of Entropy*. In these articles I discussed the laws of chemical reactions, of the dissociation of gases, and finally the properties of dilute solutions. With respect to the latter, my theory led to the conclusion that the values of the lowering of the freezing point, observed in many salt solutions, could be explained only by a dissociation of the substances dissolved, and that this finding constituted a thermodynamic foundation for the electrolytic dissociation theory advanced by Svante Arrhenius approximately at the same time. This conclusion, unfortunately, got me into an unpleasant conflict. For Arrhenius challenged, in a rather unfriendly manner, the admissibility of my arguments, pointing out that his theory related to ions, i.e. electrically charged particles. I could reply only that the laws of thermodynamics were valid regardless of whether or not the particles carried a charge.

In the spring of 1889, after the death of Kirchhoff, I accepted the invitation, extended to me upon the recommendation of the Faculty of Philosophy of Berlin, to take his place at the University, to teach theoretical physics. First, I was an associate professor, and from 1892, a full professor. These were the years of the widest expansion of my scientific outlook and way of thinking. For this was the first time that I came in closer contact with the world leaders in scientific research in those days—Helmholtz, above all the others. But I learned to know Helmholtz also as a human being, and to respect him as a man no less than I had always respected him as a scientist. For with his entire personality, integrity of convictions and modesty of character, he was the very incarnation of the dignity and probity of science. These traits of character were supplemented by a true human kindness, which touched my heart deeply. When during a conversation he would look at me with those calm, searching, penetrating, and yet so benign eyes, I would be overwhelmed by a feeling of boundless filial trust and devotion, and I would

feel that I could confide in him, without reserva-
tion, everything that I had on my mind, knowing
that I would find him a fair and tolerant judge;
and a single word of approval, let alone praise,
from his lips would make me as happy as any
worldly triumph.

I had this experience on several occasions. One
of them was when he thanked me emphatically
after my memorial address on Heinrich Hertz,
delivered before the Physical Society; another,
when he expressed his agreement with my theory
of chemical solutions, shortly before my election
to the Prussian Academy of Sciences. I shall treas-
ure the memory of every one of these thrilling
moments to the end of my days.

Besides Helmholtz, I was soon on amicable
terms with Wilhelm von Bezold, whom I had
known from Munich. Likewise, with August
Kundt, the temperamental Director of the Physical Institute, universally liked for his genuine
kind human feelings.

The other physicists were not so easy to approach. There was, for instance, Adolph Paalzow,
the physicist of the School of Engineering of
Charlottenburg, a gifted experimenter, and a

typical Berliner. He would always treat me cordially, yet always make me feel that he had really not much use for me. In those days, I was the only theorist, a physicist *sui generis,* as it were, and this circumstance did not make my *debut* so easy. Also, I had a distinct feeling that the instructors at the Physical Institute were politely but clearly trying to keep me at arm's length. But in the course of time, as we got better acquainted, our relationship assumed a friendlier aspect; one of them, Heinrich Rubens, eventually became my close personal friend, and our friendship was ended only by his death, at an all too early age.

By a sheer whim of fate, no sooner had I reported to my post in Berlin than I was temporarily assigned a task in a field quite remote from my self-chosen special branch of physics. Just at that time, the Institute for Theoretical Physics happened to receive a large harmonium, of pure untempered tuning, a product of the genius of Carl Eitz, a public school teacher in Eisleben, built by the Schiedmayer piano factory of Stuttgart for the Ministry. I was given the task of using this musical instrument for a study of the untempered, "natural" scale. I delved into the problem with keen interest, in particular with regard to the question concerning the part played by the "natural" scale in our modern vocal music without instrumental accompaniment. These studies brought me the discovery, unsuspected to a certain degree, that the tempered scale was positively more pleasing to the human ear, under all circumstances, than the "natural," untempered scale. Even in a harmonic major triad, the natural third sounds feeble and inexpressive in comparison with the tempered third. Indubitably, this fact can be ascribed ultimately to a habituation through years and generations. For before Johann Sebastian Bach, the tempered scale had not been at all universally known.

My removal to Berlin not only enabled me to associate with interesting personages, but also brought about a sizable expansion of my scientific correspondence. First of all, I became interested in the extremely fruitful theory formulated by W. Nernst, of Göttingen. According to this theory, the electric stresses occurring in electrolytic solutions with non-homogenous concentrations arise from the joint effect of the electric force, due to the moving charges and the osmotic pressure. Using this theory as a basis, I succeeded in calculating the potential difference at the point of contact of two electrolytic solutions, and Nernst wrote to me later that my formula had been confirmed by his measurements.

In connection with the problems of the electric dissociation theory, I was soon also engaged in a voluminous correspondence with Wilhelm Ostwald, of Leipzig. Our correspondence led to many a critical debate, yet these were always carried on in the friendliest tone. Ostwald, by his very nature a firm believer in systematization, distinguished three different types of energy, corresponding to the three spatial dimensions, namely: Distance Energy, Surface Energy, and Space Energy. Distance Energy, according to him, was the force of gravitation; Surface Energy, the surface tension of liquids; and Space Energy, the volume energy. I replied, among other comments, that there was no such thing as a volume energy in the sense specified by Ostwald. For instance, the energy of an ideal gas does not in fact even depend on the volume, but on the temperature of the gas. If an ideal gas is made to expand without doing any work, its volume increases, but the energy remains unchanged, whereas according to Ostwald, its energy ought to decrease with the decrease of the pressure.

Another controversy arose with relation to the question of the analogy between the passage of heat from a higher to a lower temperature and the sinking of a weight from a greater to a smaller height. I had emphasized the need for a sharp distinction between these two processes, for they differed from each other as basically as did the First and Second Laws of Thermodynamics. However, this theory of mine was contradicted by the view universally accepted in those days, and I just could not make my fellow physicists see it my way. In fact, certain physicists actually regarded Clausius' reasoning as unnecessarily complicated and even confused; and they refused, in particular, to admit the concept of irreversibility, and thereby to assign to heat a special position among the forms of energy. They created in opposition to Clausius' theory of thermodynamics, the so-called science of "Energetics." The first fundamental proposition of Energetics, exactly like that of Clausius' theory, expresses the principle of the conservation of energy; but its second proposition, which is supposed to formulate the direction of all occurrences, postulates a perfect analogy between the passing of heat from a higher to a lower temperature and the sinking of a weight from a greater to a smaller height. A consequence of this point of view was that the assumption of irreversibility for proving the Second Law of Thermodynamics was declared to be unessential; furthermore, the existence of an absolute zero of temperature was disputed, on the ground that for temperature, just as for height, only differences can be measured.

It is one of the most painful experiences of my entire scientific life that I have but seldom—in fact, I might say, never—succeeded in gaining universal recognition for a new result, the truth of which I could demonstrate by a conclusive, albeit only theoretical proof. This is what happened this time, too. All my sound arguments fell on deaf ears. It was simply impossible to be heard against the authority of men like Ostwald, Helm and Mach. I was firmly convinced that my claim of the basic difference between the transmission of heat and the sinking of a weight would eventually be proved to be right. But the annoying thing was that I was not to have at all the satisfaction of seeing myself vindicated. The universal acceptance of my thesis was ultimately brought about by considerations of an altogether different sort, unrelated to the arguments which I had adduced in support of it—namely, by the atomic theory, as represented by Ludwig Boltzmann.

Boltzmann succeeded in establishing, for a given gas in a given state, a function, H, which has the property that its value constantly decreases with time. It suffices, therefore, to identify the negative value of this H with entropy, to arrive at the principle of the increase of entropy. This discovery demonstrates, at the same time, irreversibility to be a characteristic of the processes occurring in a gas.

As events transpired, therefore, my claim concerning the fundamental difference between heat conduction and a purely mechanical process was victorious over the view previously entertained by outstanding authorities. Nevertheless, my contribution to the struggle was entirely superfluous, for even without it the outcome would have been the same.

Obviously, this battle, in which Boltzmann and

Ostwald represented the opposing views, was fought rather heatedly, and produced also many a drastic effect, for the two antagonists were each other's equals in quick repartee and natural wit. After all that I have related, in this duel of minds I could play only the part of a second to Boltzmann—a second whose services were evidently not appreciated, not even noticed, by him. For Boltzmann knew very well that my viewpoint was basically different from his. He was especially annoyed by the fact that I was not only indifferent but to a certain extent even hostile to the atomic theory which was the foundation of his entire research. The reason was that at that time, I regarded the principle of the increase of entropy as no less immutably valid than the principle of the conservation of energy itself, whereas Boltzmann treated the former merely as a law of probabilities —in other words, as a principle that could admit of exceptions. The value of function H might also increase at times. Boltzmann did not go into this point in the deduction of his "H-Theorem," and a talented pupil of mine, E. Zermelo, noted emphatically this gap in a strict proof of the theorem. In fact, Boltzmann omitted in his deduction every mention of the indispensable pre-supposition of the validity of his theorem—namely, the assumption of molecular disorder. He must have simply taken it for granted. At any rate, he answered young Zermelo in a tone of biting sarcasm, which was meant partly for me, too, for Zermelo's paper had been published with my approval. This was how Boltzmann assumed that ill-tempered tone which he continued to exhibit toward me, on later occasions as well, both in his publications and in our personal correspondence; and it was only in the last years of his life, when I informed him of the atomistic foundation for my radiation law, that he assumed a friendlier attitude.

Boltzmann eventually triumphed in the fight against Ostwald and the adherents of Energetics, as it had been self-evident to me that he would, in view of all that I have just mentioned. The basic difference between the conduction of heat and a purely mechanical process became universally recognized. This experience gave me also an opportunity to learn a fact—a remarkable one, in my opinion: A new scientific truth does not triumph by convincing its opponents and making them see the light, but rather because its opponents eventually die, and a new generation grows up that is familiar with it.

Otherwise, the controversies just mentioned held comparatively little interest for me, as they could not be expected to produce anything new. My attention, therefore, was soon claimed by quite another problem, which was to dominate me and urge me on to a great many different investigations for a long time to come. The measurements made by O. Lummer and E. Pringsheim in the German Physico-Technical Institute, in connection with the study of the thermal spectrum, directed my attention to Kirchhoff's Law, which says that in an evacuated cavity, bounded by totally reflecting walls, and containing any arbitrary number of emitting and absorbing bodies, in time a state will be reached where all bodies have the same temperature, and the radiation, in all its properties including its spectral energy distribution, depends not on the nature of the bodies, but solely and exclusively on the temperature. Thus, this so-called Normal Spectral Energy Distribution represents something absolute, and since I had always regarded the search for the absolute as the loftiest goal of all scientific activity, I eagerly set to work. I found a direct method for solving the problem in the application of Maxwell's Electromagnetic Theory of Light. Namely, I assumed the cavity to be filled with simple linear oscillators or resonators, subject to small damping forces and having different periods; and I expected the exchange of energy caused by the reciprocal radiation of the oscillators to result, in time, in a stationary state of the normal energy distribution corresponding to Kirchhoff's Law.

This extended series of investigations, certain ones of which could be verified by comparisons with known observational data, such as the measurements of damping by V. Bjerknes, resulted in establishing the general relationship between the energy of an oscillator having a definite period, and the energy radiation of the corresponding spectral region in the surrounding field when the exchange of energy is stationary. From this there followed the remarkable result that this relationship is absolutely independent of the damping constant of the oscillator—a circumstance which was very pleasing and welcome to me, because it permitted the entire problem to be simplified, by substituting the energy of the oscillator for the energy of the radiation, thus replacing a complicated structure possessing many degrees of freedom, by a simple system with just one degree of freedom.

To be sure, this result represented a mere preliminary to the tackling of the real problem, which now loomed all the more formidably before me. My first attempt to overcome it was unsuccessful, for my original silent hope that the radiation emitted by the oscillator would differ, in some characteristic way, from the absorbed radiation, turned out to have been mere wishful thinking. The oscillator reacts only to those rays which it is capable of emitting, and is completely insensitive to adjacent spectral regions.

Moreover, my suggestion that the oscillator was capable of exerting a unilateral, in other words irreversible, effect on the energy of the surrounding field, drew a vigorous protest from Boltzmann, who, with his wider experience in this domain, demonstrated that according to the laws of classical dynamics, each of the processes I considered could also take place in the opposite direction; and indeed in such a manner, that a spherical wave emitted by an oscillator could reverse its direction of motion, contract progressively until it reached the oscillator and be reabsorbed by the latter, so that the oscillator could then again emit the previously absorbed energy in the same direction from which the energy had been received. To be sure, I could exclude such odd phenomena as inwardly directed spherical waves, by the introduction of a specific stipulation—the hypothesis of a natural radiation, which plays the same part in the theory of radiation as the hypothesis of molecular disorder in the kinetic theory of gases, in that it guarantees the irreversibility of the radiation processes. But the calculations showed ever more clearly that an essential link was still missing, without which the attack on the core of the entire problem could not be undertaken successfully.

So I had no other alternative than to tackle the problem once again—this time from the opposite side, namely, from the side of thermodynamics, my own home territory where I felt myself to be on safer ground. In fact, my previous studies of the Second Law of Thermodynamics came to

stand me in good stead now, for at the very outset
I hit upon the idea of correlating not the temperature but the entropy of the oscillator with its
energy. It was an odd jest of fate that a circumstance which on former occasions I had found
unpleasant, namely, the lack of interest of my
colleagues in the direction taken by my investigations, now turned out to be an outright boon.
While a host of outstanding physicists worked on
the problem of spectral energy distribution, both
from the experimental and theoretical aspect,
every one of them directed his efforts solely
toward exhibiting the dependence of the intensity
of radiation on the temperature. On the other
hand, I suspected that the fundamental connection lies in the dependence of entropy upon
energy. As the significance of the concept of entropy had not yet come to be fully appreciated,
nobody paid any attention to the method adopted
by me, and I could work out my calculations completely at my leisure, with absolute thoroughness,
without fear of interference or competition.

Since for the irreversibility of the exchange of
energy between an oscillator and the radiation
activating it, the second differential quotient of

its entropy with respect to its energy is of characteristic significance, I calculated the value of this function on the assumption that Wien's Law of the Spectral Energy Distribution is valid—a law which was then in the focus of general interest; I got the remarkable result that on this assumption the reciprocal of that value, which I shall call here R, is proportional to the energy. This relationship is so surprisingly simple that for a while I considered it to possess universal validity, and I endeavored to prove it theoretically. However, this view soon proved to be untenable in the face of later measurements. For although in the case of small energies and correspondingly short waves Wien's Law continued to be confirmed in a satisfactory manner, in the case of large values of the energy and correspondingly long waves, appreciable divergences were found, first by Lummer and Pringsheim; and finally the measurements of H. Rubens and F. Kurlbaum on infrared rays of fluorspar and rock-salt revealed a behavior which, though totally different, is again a simple one, in so far as the function R is proportional not to the energy but to the square of the energy for large values of the energy and wave-lengths.

Thus, direct experiments established two simple limits for the function R: For small energies, R is proportional to the energy; for larger energy values R is proportional to the square of the energy. Obviously, just as every principle of spectral energy distribution yields a certain value for R, so also every formula for R leads to a definite law of the distribution of energy. The problem was to find such a formula for R which would result in the law of the distribution of energy established by measurements. Therefore, the most obvious step for the general case was to make the value of R equal to the sum of a term proportional to the first power of the energy and another term proportional to the second power of the energy, so that the first term becomes decisive for small values of the energy and the second term for large values. In this way a new radiation formula was obtained, and I submitted it for examination to the Berlin Physical Society, at the meeting on October 19, 1900.

The very next morning, I received a visit from my colleague Rubens. He came to tell me that after the conclusion of the meeting he had that very night checked my formula against the results of his measurements, and found a satisfactory concordance at every point. Also Lummer and Pringsheim, who first thought to have discovered divergences, soon withdrew their objections; for, as Pringsheim related it to me, the observed divergences turned out to have been due to an error in calculation. Later measurements, too, confirmed my radiation formula again and again, —the finer the methods of measurement used, the more accurate the formula was found to be.

But even if the absolutely precise validity of the radiation formula is taken for granted, so long as it had merely the standing of a law disclosed by a lucky intuition, it could not be expected to possess more than a formal significance. For this reason, on the very day when I formulated this law, I began to devote myself to the task of investing it with a true physical meaning. This quest automatically led me to study the interrelation of entropy and probability—in other words, to pursue the line of thought inaugurated by Boltzmann. Since the entropy S is an additive magnitude but the probability W is a multiplicative one, I simply postulated that $S = k \cdot \log W$, where k is a universal constant; and I investigated whether the formula for W, which is obtained when S is replaced by its value corresponding to the above radiation law, could be interpreted as a measure of probability.

As a result,* I found that this was actually possible, and that in this connection k represents the so-called absolute gas constant, referred not to gram-molecules or mols, but to the real molecules. It is, understandably, often called *Boltzmann's constant*. However, this calls for the comment that Boltzmann never introduced this constant, nor, to the best of my knowledge, did he ever think of investigating its numerical value. For had he done so, he would have had to examine the matter of the number of the real atoms —a task, however, which he left to his colleague J. Loschmidt, while he, in his own calculations, always kept in sight the possibility that the kinetic theory of gases represents only a mechanical picture. He was therefore satisfied with stopping at the gram-atoms. The letter k has won acceptance

* This finding, containing the introduction of the ultimate energy quanta for the oscillator, was reported by Max Planck again before the Physical Society of Berlin on December 14, 1900. That was the birthday of the Quantum Theory. (*Max von Laue*)

only gradually. Even several years after its introduction, it was still customary to calculate with
the Loschmidt number L.

Now as for the magnitude W, I found that in
order to interpret it as a probability, it was necessary to introduce a universal constant, which I
called h. Since it had the dimension of action
(energy $\times$ time), I gave it the name, *elementary
quantum of action*. Thus the nature of entropy as
a measure of probability, in the sense indicated
by Boltzmann, was established in the domain of
radiation, too. This was made especially clear in
a proposition, the validity of which my closest
pupil, Max von Laue, convinced me in a number
of conversations—namely, that the entropy of two
coherent pencils of light is smaller than the sum
of the entropies of the individual pencils of rays,
quite consistently with the proposition that the
probability of the happening of two mutually interdependent reactions is different from the
product of the individual reactions.

While the significance of the quantum of action
for the interrelation between entropy and probability was thus conclusively established, the part
played by this new constant in the uniformly reg-

ular occurrence of physical processes still remained an open question. I therefore, tried immediately to weld the elementary quantum of action h somehow into the framework of the classical theory. But in the face of all such attempts, this constant showed itself to be obdurate. So long as it could be regarded as infinitesimally small, i.e. when dealing with higher energies and longer periods of time, everything was in perfect order. But in the general case difficulties would arise at one point or another, difficulties which became more noticeable as higher frequencies were taken into· consideration. The failure of every attempt to bridge this obstacle soon made it evident that the elementary quantum of action plays a fundamental part in atomic physics, and that its introduction opened up a new era in natural science. For it heralded the advent of something entirely unprecedented, and was destined to remodel basically the physical outlook and thinking of man which, ever since Leibniz and Newton laid the groundwork for infinitesimal calculus, were founded on the assumption that all causal interactions are continuous.

My futile attempts to fit the elementary quantum of action somehow into the classical theory continued for a number of years, and they cost me a great deal of effort. Many of my colleagues saw in this something bordering on a tragedy. But I feel differently about it. For the thorough enlightenment I thus received was all the more valuable. I now knew for a fact that the elementary quantum of action played a far more significant part in physics than I had originally been inclined to suspect, and this recognition made me see clearly the need for the introduction of totally new methods of analysis and reasoning in the treatment of atomic problems. The development of such methods—in which, however, I could no longer take an active part—was advanced mainly by the efforts of Niels Bohr and Erwin Schrödinger. Bohr, with his atom model and Correspondence Principle, laid the foundation for a reasonable unification of quantum theory with classical theory. Schrödinger, through his differential equation, created wave mechanics, and thereby the dualism between wave and particle.

I have just described how the quantum theory came gradually to occupy the focus of my interest in the field of physics. Eventually, it had to share this prominent position with another principle, which introduced me to a new sphere of ideas. In 1905, Albert Einstein published a paper in the *Annalen der Physik* which contained the basic ideas of the Theory of Relativity, and my acute interest in their development was immediately roused.

In order to preclude a likely misunderstanding, I have to insert here a few explanatory remarks of general character. In the opening paragraph of this autobiographical sketch, I emphasized that I had always looked upon the search for the absolute as the noblest and most worth while task of science. The reader might consider this contradictory to my avowed interest in the Theory of Relativity. But it would be fundamentally erroneous to look at it that way. For everything that is relative presupposes the existence of something that is absolute, and is meaningful only when juxtaposed to something absolute. The often-heard phrase, "Everything is relative," is both misleading and thoughtless. The Theory of Relativity, too, is based on something absolute, namely, the determination of the matrix of the space-time continuum; and it is an especially stimulating undertaking to discover the absolute which alone makes meaningful something given as relative.

Our every starting-point must necessarily be something relative. All our measurements are relative. The material that goes into our instruments varies according to its geographic source; their construction depends on the skill of the designer and toolmaker; their manipulation is contingent on the special purposes pursued by the experimenter. Our task is to find in all these factors and data, the absolute, the universally valid, the invariant, that is hidden in them,

This applies to the Theory of Relativity, too. I was attracted by the problem of deducing from its propositions that which served as their absolute immutable foundation. The way in which this was accomplished, was comparatively simple. In the first place, the Theory of Relativity confers an absolute meaning on a magnitude which in classical theory has only a relative significance: the velocity of light. The velocity of light is to the Theory of Relativity as the elementary quantum of action is to the Quantum Theory: it is its absolute core. In this connection, it turns out that a general principle of classical theory, the least-action principle, is also invariant with respect to the Theory of Relativity; accordingly, the quantum of action retains its significance in the Theory of Relativity as well.

This was what I tried to establish in all details, first for point masses, and then for black-body radiation. These researches yielded, among other results, the inertia of radiation and the invariance of entropy in systems possessing relative velocities.

But this is not all. The absolute showed itself to be even more deeply rooted in the order of natural laws than had been assumed for a long time. In 1906, W. Nernst came out with his heat theorem, often referred to as the "Third Law of Thermodynamics." As I immediately established, it amounted to the hypothesis that entropy, until then defined only up to an additive constant, possessed an absolute positive value. This value, from which all equations of equilibrium follow, can be calculated beforehand. In the case of a chemically homogeneous solid or liquid (in other words, a solid or liquid composed of homogeneous molecules) of which the absolute temperature is zero, this value is likewise zero. This principle in itself expresses an important fact, namely that the specific heat of a solid or liquid vanishes at the absolute zero of temperature. For other temperatures, fruitful inferences follow, with respect to the melting points of a body and the transition temperature of allotropic changes. If now one passes from chemically homogeneous solids and liquids to bodies with heterogeneous molecules, or to solutions and gases, the absolute entropy is calculated by means of combinatory considerations, in which the elementary quantum of action, too, must be included. In this way one can obtain the chemical properties of any given body, and thus a complete answer is found to all problems dealing with physico-chemical equilibrium. However, in questions concerned with the temporal developments of processes other forces must be taken into account, and problems about such forces are not resolved by considering the value of the entropy.

Even though as a consequence of my advancing age I have been able to take an increasingly smaller direct part in scientific research, there was compensation for this in the considerable expansion of my scientific correspondence, which I found enormously stimulating and invigorating. In this respect, I would like to mention, in particular, my correspondence with Cl. Schaefer, whose *Introduction to Theoretical Physics* I consider as pedagogically unexcelled. Our correspondence concerned his presentation of the Second Law of Thermodynamics. I also carried on an interesting correspondence with A. Sommerfeld, on the problem of the quantization of systems with several degrees of freedom. This particular correspondence even culminated in a final exchange of poetic tributes, which I shall take the liberty to quote here, although I must demur in all fairness that Sommerfeld seriously underestimated his own achievements in this field. This is how he referred to my studies on the structures of phase space:

> *You cultivate the virgin soil,*
> *Where picking flowers was my only toil.*

My only possible reply was:

> *You picked flowers—well, so have I.*
> *Let them be, then, combined;*

AND OTHER PAPERS

Let us exchange our flowers fair,
And in the brightest wreath them bind.

I have satisfied my inner need for bearing witness, as fully as possible, both to the results of my scientific labors and to my gradually crystallized attitude to general questions—such as the meaning of exact science, its relationship to religion, the connection between causality and free will—by always complying willingly with the ever increasing number of invitations to deliver lectures before Academies, Universities, learned societies, and before the general public, and these lectures have been the source of a many a valuable personal stimulation which I shall gratefully cherish in loving memory for the rest of my life.

Phantom Problems in Science *

The world is teeming with problems. Wherever man looks, some new problem crops up to meet his eye—in his home life as well as in his business or professional activity, in the realm of economics as well as in the field of technology, in the arts as well as in science. And some problems are very stubborn; they just refuse to let us in peace. Our agonized thinking of them may sometimes reach such a pitch that our thoughts haunt us throughout the day, and even rob us of sleep at night. And if by lucky chance we succeed in solving a problem, we experience a sense of deliverance, and rejoice over the enrichment of our knowledge. But it is an entirely different story, and an experience annoying as can be, to find after a long time spent in toil and effort, that the problem which has been preying on one's mind

* A Lecture delivered by Max Planck in Göttingen on June 17, 1946.

is totally incapable of any solution at all—either because there exists no indisputable method to unravel it, or because considered in the cold light of reason, it turns out to be absolutely void of all meaning—in other words, it is a *phantom problem,* and all that mental work and effort was expended on a mere nothing. There are many such phantom problems—in my opinion, far more than one would ordinarily suspect—even in the realm of science.

There is no better safeguard against such unpleasant experiences than to ascertain in each instance, and at the very outset, whether the problem under consideration is a genuine or meaningful one, and whether a solution for it is to be expected. In view of this situation I will cite and examine a number of problems, in order to see whether they happen to be mere phantom problems. By doing so, I may be able to render a genuinely useful service to some of you. My selection of these problems to be exhibited as specimens is not based on any systematic viewpoint, and even less can it lay a claim to completeness in any respect. Most of them are taken from the realm of science, because this is the field in which the relevant factors are the most clearly discernible. However, this consideration will not deter me from touching upon other fields, too, whenever I can reasonably surmise that the subject holds an interest for you.

I.

In order to decide whether or not a given problem is truly meaningful, we must first of all examine closely the assumptions contained in its wording. In many instances, these alone will immediately reveal the problem under consideration to be a phantom problem. The matter is simplest when an error is lurking in the assumptions. In this case, of course, it is immaterial whether the erroneous assumption was introduced deliberately or has just escaped detection. A lucid example is the famous problem of perpetual motion, i.e. the problem of devising a periodically functioning apparatus which will perform mechanical work perpetually without any other change in nature. Since the existence of such an apparatus would contradict the principle of the conservation of energy, such an apparatus cannot possibly occur in nature, so that this problem is a phantom problem. Of course, one may raise the following argument: "The principle of the conservation of energy, after all, is an experimental law. Accordingly, although today it is considered to be universal and all-embracing, its validity may one day have to be restricted—and in fact, such a curtailment of its universal applicability has been sometimes suspected in nuclear physics—and the problem of perpetual motion would then suddenly become genuine. Its meaninglessness is, therefore, by no means absolute."

This counter-argument may actually acquire practical significance, as is demonstrated especially clearly by the example of a no less well-known problem in chemistry: The ancient problem of changing base metal, for instance, mercury, into gold. Originally, prior to the birth of a scientific chemistry, this problem was considered to be pregnant with portentious meaning, and many a learned—and unlearned—mind was zealously occupied with it. But later, as the theory of chemical elements was developed and became universally accepted, the transmutation of metals turned into a phantom problem. In recent times, since the discovery of artificial radioactivity, the situation has again been reversed. The fact is that today it no longer seems to be fundamentally impossible to discover a process for removing a proton from the nucleus of the mercury atom and an electron from its shell. This operation would change the mercury atom into a gold atom. Therefore, at the present stage of science, the ancient quest of the alchemists no longer belongs to the class of phantom problems.

However, these examples must by no means be construed as indicating that the meaninglessness of a phantom problem is never absolute, but simply dependent on whether or not a certain theory is accepted as valid. There are also many phantom problems which are indubitably doomed to remain such forever. One of these, for instance, is the problem which used to keep many a great physicist busy for many years: The study of the mechanical properties of the luminiferous ether. The meaninglessness of this problem follows from its basic premise, which postulates that light vibrations are of a mechanical nature. This premise is erroneous, and must so remain forever.

Here is another example, taken from the field of physiology: It is a well known fact that the convex lens of the human eye projects an inverted image on the retina. When we see a tower, its image appears on the retina with the top of the tower pointing downward. When this phenomenon was established, a number of scientists tried to detect in the human organ of sight that particular mechanism which supposedly re-inverts the image on the retina. This is a phantom problem, and never can be anything else, for it is based on an erroneous premise, for which there can be no possible proof—namely, that in the organ of vision the image of an object must be upright rather than inverted.

Far more difficult than those cases in which, as in the examples just cited, the assumptions are mistaken, are problems whose presuppositions contain no error, but are so vaguely worded that they must remain phantom ones because they are inadequately formulated. Yet, it so happens that it is just such cases with which we shall be chiefly preoccupied.

My first example is a phantom problem, for the triviality of which I beg your forgiveness. The room in which we now sit, has two side walls, a right-hand one and a left-hand one. To you, *this* is the right side, to me, sitting facing you, *that* is the right side. The problem is: Which side is in reality the right-hand one? I know that this question sounds ridiculous, yet I dare call it typical of an entire host of problems which have been, and in part still are, the subject of earnest and learned debates, except that the situation is not always quite so clear. It demonstrates, right at the very outset, what great caution must be exercised in using the word, *real*. In many instances, the word has any sense at all only when the speaker first defines clearly the point of view on which his considerations are based. Otherwise, the words, *real* or *reality,* are often empty and misleading.

Another example: I see a star shining in the sky. What is *real* in it? Is it the glowing substance, of which it is composed, or is it the sensation of light in my eyes? The question is meaningless so long as I do not state whether I am assuming a realistic or a positivistic point of view.

Still another example, this one from the realm of modern physics: When the behavior of a moving electron is studied through an electron microscope, the electron appears as a particle following a definite course. But when the electron is made to pass through a crystal, the image projected on the screen shows every characteristic of a refracted light wave. The question, whether the electron is in reality a particle, occupying a certain position in space at a certain time, or a wave, filling all of infinite space, will therefore constitute a phantom problem so long as we fail to stipulate which of the two viewpoints is applied in the study of the behavior of the electron.

The famous controversy between Newton's emission theory and Huygens' wave theory of light is also a phantom problem of science. For every decision for or against either of these two opposing theories will be a completely arbitrary one, depending on whether one accepts the point of view of the quantum theory or that of the classical theory.

II.

In every one of the cases cited till now, we encountered a rather simple, easily appreciable situation. Now let us proceed to the consideration of a problem which has always regarded as one of central importance because of its meaning to human life—the famous body-mind problem. In this case, first of all we must try to ascertain the meaning of our problem. For there are philosophers who claim that mental processes need not be accompanied by physical processes at all, but can take place totally independently from the latter. If this view is right, mental processes are subject to entirely different laws than those applying to physical processes. If so, then, the body-mind problems splits into two separate problems—the body problem and the mind problem—thus losing its meaning, and degenerating into a phantom problem. With this finding, the case may be considered as good as closed, and we need only concern ourselves with the reciprocal interaction of mental and physical processes. Experience shows that they are very closely influenced by each other. For instance, somebody asks me a question. His question is introduced by a physical process, the propagation of the sound waves of the spoken words which, emitted by him, hit my ears and are transmitted to my brain through the sensory nerve paths. They then cause mental processes to take place in my brain, namely, a reflection on the meaning of the words perceived, followed by a decision as to the content of the answer to be given. Then another physical process operates my motor nerves and my larynx, to transmit the answer to the questioner by means of the physical process of propagating sound waves through the air.

Now then, what is the nature of the interrelation of physical and mental processes? Are mental processes caused by physical ones? And if so, according to what laws? How can something material act on something immaterial, and *vice versa?* All these questions are difficult to answer. If we assume the existence of a causal interaction, a cause-and-effect relationship, between physical and mental processes, a continued, unrestricted applicability of the principle of the conservation of energy appears to be an indispensable premise. For one will not be disposed to sacrifice this universal foundation of exact science. But in that case, there would have to exist a numerically definite mechanical equivalent of psychic processes, as there is a definite equivalent of heat in thermodynamics, and there would be absolutely no method for measuring such a constant. For this reason, a solution has been attempted on the basis of the hypothesis that the mental forces contribute no perceptible energy to the physical processes, but act merely to liberate the latter, as a gentle breeze will start something that will grow into a mighty avalanche, or a tiny spark will blow up a huge powder magazine. However, this hypothesis does not solve the difficulty completely. Because in every case known to us, while the amount of energy expanded in liberating a process is very small in comparison with the energy released, yet it does exist, even though it may have just a microscopic magnitude. Even the very gentlest breeze and very tiniest spark possess an energy above zero—and this is what matters here.

However, it is well known that there are some forces which produce a perceptible effect without any expenditure whatever of energy. These are what we may call "guiding forces," such as, for instance, the resistance due to the rigidity of railroad rails which forces the wheels of a train to follow a pre-determined curve, without any expenditure of energy. An attempt might be made to ascribe a similar role to the mental forces in the guiding of physical processes along pre-determined paths in the human brain. But this, too, involves grave and insurmountable difficulties. For the modern science of brain physiology is based on the very premise that it is possible to achieve a satisfactory understanding of the laws of biological processes without postulating the intervention of any particular mental force. Such a hypothesis avoids also the theory of parallelism which, in contrast to the theory of interaction, assumes that mental and physical processes must, necessarily, run side by side, each according to its own laws, without interfering with each other. Of course, it still remains incomprehensible just how this reciprocal interdependence of two such fundamentally different occurrences is to be conceived, and whether it perhaps requires the assumption of some form of pre-established harmony. In this respect, the theory of parallelism, too, is hardly satisfactory.

And now, in order to get to the bottom of the matter, let us ask ourselves this question of basic significance: Just what do we know about mental processes? In what circumstances and in what sense may we speak of mental processes? Let us

consider first where we come across mental processes in this world. We must take it for granted
that members of the higher animal kingdom as
well as human beings have emotions and sensations. But as we descend to the lower animals—
where is the borderline where sensation ceases to
exist? Has a worm any sensation of pain as it is
crushed under our feet? And may plants be considered capable of some kind of sensation? There
are botanists who are disposed to answer this
question affirmatively. But such a theory can
never be put to the test, let alone proved, and the
wisest course seems to be not to venture any opinion in this regard. Along the entire ladder of evo-
lution, from the lowest order of life up to Man,
there is no point at which one can establish a
discontinuity in the nature of mental processes.

It is nevertheless possible to specify a quite definite borderline, of decisive importance for all
that follows. This is the borderline between the
mental processes within other individuals and the
mental processes within one's own Ego. For everybody experiences his own emotions and sensations
directly. They just simply exist for him. But we
do not experience directly the sensations of any

other individuals, however certain their existence may be, and we can only infer them in analogy to our own sensations. To be sure, there are physicians who solemnly claim to be able to perceive the emotions and moods of their patients no less clearly than the latter themselves. But such a claim can never be proved indisputably. Its questionability becomes most striking if we think of certain specific instances. Even the most sensitive dentist cannot feel the piercing pains which his patient at times has to suffer under his treatment. He can ascertain them only indirectly, on the basis of the moans or squirming of the patient. Or, to speak of a more pleasant situation, such as for instance a banquet, however clearly one may sense the pleasure of one's neighbor over the taste of his favorite wine, it is something quite different from tasting it on one's own tongue. What *you* feel, think, want, only *you* can know as firsthand information. Other people can conclude it only indirectly, from your words, conduct, actions and mannerisms. When such physical manifestations are entirely absent, they have no basis whatever to enable them to know your momentary mental state.

This contrast between first-hand, or direct, and second-hand, or indirect, experience is a fundamental one. Since our primary aim is to gain direct, first-hand experience, we shall now discuss the interrelation of our mental and physical states.

First of all, we find that we may speak of conscious states only. To be sure, many processes, perhaps even the most decisive ones, must be taking place in the subconscious mind. But these are beyond the reach of scientific analysis. For there exists no science of the unconscious, or subconscious, mind. It would be a contradiction in terms, a self-contradiction. One does not know that which is subconscious. Therefore, all problems concerning the subconscious are phantom problems.

Let us therefore take a simple conscious process involving body and mind. I prick my hand with a needle, and feel a sensation of pain. The wound made by the pin is the physical element, the sensation of pain is the mental element of the process. The wound is seen, the pain is felt. Is there, then, an indisputable method of throwing light upon the interrelation of the two elements of this process? It is easy to realize that this is absolutely impossible. For there is nothing here upon which light is to be thrown. The visual perception of the wound and the feeling of the pain are elementary facts of experience, but they are as different in nature as knowledge and feeling. Therefore, the question as to their essential interrelation represents no meaningful problem—it is just a phantom problem.

It is obvious that the two occurrences, the pinprick and the sensation of pain, can be examined and analyzed most thoroughly, in every detail. But such an analysis calls for two different methods, which mutually preclude each other. Each of the two corresponds to one of two different viewpoints. In the following I will refer to them, respectively, as the *psychological* and the *physiological* viewpoints. Observation based on the psychological viewpoint is rooted in self-consciousness; therefore, it is applicable directly only to the analysis of one's own mental processes. On the other hand, observation based on the physiological viewpoint is directed at the processes in the external world; therefore, its direct scope is limited to physical processes. These two viewpoints are incompatible. The adoption of one when the other one is called for, always leads to confusion. We cannot judge our mental processes directly from the physiological viewpoint any more than we can examine a physical process from the psychological viewpoint. This state of affairs makes the body-mind problem appear in a different light. For the examination of psychosomatic processes will yield entirely different results, according as the psychological or the physiological viewpoint is taken as the basis of observation. The psychological viewpoint will permit us to gain first-hand knowledge solely and exclusively of something that relates to our mental processes. The physiological viewpoint will produce first-hand information about physical processes only. It is therefore impossible to gain first-hand information about both physical and mental processes from any single viewpoint; and since in order to reach a clear conclusion, we must adhere to a given viewpoint, which automatically excludes the other, the search for the interrelation of physical and mental processes loses its meaning. In this case, there exist only physical processes *or* mental processes, but never processes which are physical *and* mental.

Therefore, it will do no harm to say that the physical and the mental are in no way different from each other. They are the selfsame processes, only viewed from two diametrically opposite directions. This statement is the answer to the riddle, which has been inseparable from the theory of parallelism, namely, how one is to conceive the fact that two types of processes so different from each other as the physical and the mental, are so closely interlinked. The link has now been disclosed. At the same time, the body-mind problem has been recognized as another phantom problem.

III.

The cases heretofore discussed have dealt only with knowledge, and feeling. Physical states and processes are known, mental states and processes are felt. The situation is quite different, and more complicated, when cognition and feeling are joined by volition. For in that case we are confronted by the ancient dilemma of freedom of the will *versus* the law of causality. This problem holds a certain significance for ethics, too, and its discussion will be our immediate next step.

Is the will free, or is it causally determined? In order to be able to answer this question, first of all we must examine the methods which can be utilized for the study of the laws and regularity of volitional processes.

In this connection an important point must first be observed: In order to gain a correct insight into the regular course of a process, one must take every precaution lest the process be influenced by the method of observation used. Thus, for instance, when trying to ascertain the temperature of a body, we must not use any thermometer, the introduction of which would cause a change in the temperature under examination; similarly, in the microscopic observation of the processes taking place in a living cell, we must not employ illumination which might interfere with the normal course of those processes. All that holds true for physical and biological processes, applies naturally to the same extent to mental states and processes, too. It is one of the most elementary principles of experimental psychology that an observation may produce a totally false finding if the subject knows, or even suspects that he is being observed. For this reason, under certain circumstances, the observation itself will constitute a serious source of error.

Applying the above principle to the problem now before us, the most basic and elementary requirement which a scientifically perfect observation of the regular course of a volitional impulse must fulfill, is that it should not affect or influence that impulse. The automatic consequence of this requirement is that the choice of the acceptable viewpoint of the observation must, necessarily, be restricted. Namely, since the observation itself is no less a mental process than the volitional impulse which is to be observed, the observation may, under certain circumstances, influence the course of the volitional impulse, and thus distort the final finding. The only time when there is no reason to fear such interference is when you observe the will of another person without his knowledge, or when another person observes your will without your knowledge. On the other hand, this source of error will always be operative whenever you attempt to observe your own will. For in that case the mental process of the observation coincides in your unified self-consciousness with the mental process of the volitional impulse. Therefore, it is inadmissible to observe one's own will from the viewpoint of one's own Ego—and I am referring to the present as well as the future act of will, for the latter is co-determined by the present will, too. On the other hand, there is nothing to preclude a scientific observation of a volitional impulse of one's own past Ego. For past mental processes are not affected by a later analysis. In order to express this situation, I shall from now on make a distinction between an external and an internal viewpoint of observation. The external viewpoint is the one which permits the volitional processes to be observed without being disturbed, affected, or interfered with, by the observation. This viewpoint is adopted when observing the volitional processes of others, as well as when observing the *past* volitional processes of one's own Ego. The internal viewpoint is the one, from which the volitional processes cannot be observed without being thereby disturbed. This viewpoint is adopted when observing the present and future volitional processes of one's own Ego. The external viewpoint is suitable for a scientific examination of the laws governing volitional processes; the internal viewpoint is not admissible for this purpose. It is self-evident that these two viewpoints mutually preclude each other, and that it is senseless to apply both of them simultaneously.

Now then, if we adopt the external viewpoint —the only one admissible—as the basis of our scientific observation of volitional processes, every-day experience tells us that in our daily dealings with others we always presuppose certain motives, in other words, a causal determinism, in whatever they say and do, for otherwise their behavior would be inaccountable, and any orderly contact with them would be impossible. The same principle applies to scientific research, too. If a historian wanted to ascribe the decision of Julius Caesar to cross the Rubicon not to his political deliberations and to his innate temperament, but to free will, his view would be tantamount to a renunciation of scientific understanding. Therefore, we will have to conclude that from the external viewpoint of observation the will is to be assumed as causally determined.

The state of affairs is quite different as regards

the internal viewpoint. As we have seen, the scientific method of observation fails to work here. On the other hand, however, this viewpoint opens up another source of information: Self-consciousness, which tells us immediately that we are able at any time to give any desired turn to our will as we can to our thoughts, whether as a result of mature deliberation, discretion, or even sheer whim. In this connection, it must be observed that this is by no means a matter of an overt volitional act, which is often impeded by external circumstances, but solely giving the will an intended direction. In this domain we have absolute supreme command. Just think of the unspoken mental reservations which we are able to make with every word we speak. This is a real freedom, experienced at first hand, not a make-believe freedom, as it is claimed by many people who are unable to keep distinct the two opposite viewpoints. Of course, he who seeks to know the "real" freedom of will without reference to the viewpoint adopted, proceeds no differently than does the one who asks without further specification which side of this room is "really" the right side. On the present analysis, neither does the freedom of the will rest, as some have supposed, on a certain lack of intelligence. The degree of intelligence is of absolutely no significance here. Even the most intelligent person is no more capable of observing himself from the outside than is even the fastest runner of passing himself.

In summary, we can therefore say: Observed from without, the will is causally determined. Observed from within, it is free. This finding takes care of the problem of the freedom of the will. This problem came into being because people were not careful enough to specify explicitly the viewpoint of the observation, and to adhere to it consistently. This is a typical example of a phantom problem. Even though this truth is still being disputed time and again, there is no doubt in my mind that it is but a question of time before it will gain universal recognition.

IV.

There are many more examples that can be cited to illustrate what grave consequences may be entailed by an improper confusion of two opposite viewpoints. Let us consider one more particularly frequent case, the confusion of the scientific viewpoint with the religious viewpoint. Even though science and religion, in their ultimate effects, are headed for the same goal, the recognition of an omnipotent intellect ruling the universe, yet they are basically different both in their starting points and methods. And in order to attain fruitful results, one must be careful to study a given problem from the suitable viewpoint, which must then be consistently followed. Unfortunately, up to this time, this requirement has often been totally disregarded. In fact, inquiries often switch abruptly from one perspective to the other. This error is being committed by both sides; in other words, one often finds the scientific viewpoint improperly applied to the treatment of ethico-religious questions, and also considerations of religious character dragged into purely scientific problems. The first case is illustrated by the above discussion of the consciousness of freedom, which recent attempts have endeavored to reduce to the breakdown of the law of causality in modern physics, although it has nothing in the least to do with the law of causality. The repeated efforts to establish scientific grounds for the existence and personality of God stand on the same level. The other side of the picture is exemplified by the violent battle of the Church in past ages against the Copernican view of the universe, or in recent times by the campaign against the physical theory of relativity, on the basis of emotional attitudes and political arguments, which have nothing to do with science.

In this matter, a fundamental and serious dilemma must, however, be faced. If so many instances indicate that great and important questions are revealed to be phantom problems on careful analysis, that in fact the very word, *real*, often has a meaning which varies with the standpoint adopted—does not scientific knowledge reduce to a plain relativism? Is there, then, no absolutely valid view, no absolute reality, independent of any special perspective?

It would be unfortunate indeed if this were so. No—there must exist, in science, too, absolutely correct and final maxims, just as there are absolute values in ethics. Moreover, and this is the main thing, these very propositions, maxims and values are the most important and worth while goals of every endeavor. In the realm of exact science, there are the values of the *absolute con-*

stants, such as the elementary quantum of electricity, or the elementary quantum of action, and many others. These constants always prove to be the same, regardless of the method used for measuring them. The endeavor to discover them and to trace all physical and chemical processes back to them, is the very thing that may be called the ultimate goal of scientific research and study.

Nor is the situation different in the world of religion and ethics. To be sure, there, too, a considerable role is often played by the viewpoint that is adopted as a consequence of the special conditions involved in a given problem. Thus, the moral standard of truthfulness often appears to be loosened and weakened in a regrettable manner. I want to disregard here completely the conventional lies to which people resort for the sake of social amenities. But truthfulness, this noblest of all human virtues, is authoritative even here over a well-defined domain, within which its moral commandment acquires an absolute meaning, independent of all specific viewpoints. This is probity to one's own self, before one's own conscience. Under no circumstances can there be in this domain the slightest moral compromise, the slightest moral justification for the smallest deviation. He who violates this commandment, perhaps in the endeavor to gain some momentary worldly advantage, by deliberately and knowingly shutting his eyes to the proper evaluation of the true situation, like a spendthrift who thoughtlessly squanders away his wealth, and who must inevitably suffer, sooner or later, the grave consequences of his foolhardiness.

These absolute values in science and ethics are the ones whose pursuit constitutes the true task of every intellectually alert and active human being, a task which confronts all men again and again, in one form or another. This task is never finished—a fact guaranteed by the circumstance that genuine problems, even though sometimes accompanied by phantom problems, constantly appear in ceaseless variety and constantly set new tasks for active human beings. For it is work which is the favorable wind that makes the ship of human life sail the high seas, and as for the evaluation of the worth of this work, there is an infallible, time-honored measure, a phrase which pronounces the final, authoritative judgment for all times: *By their fruits ye shall know them!*

The Meaning and Limits of Exact Science *

EXACT SCIENCE—what wealth of connotation these two words have! They conjure up a vision of a lofty structure, of imperishable slabs of stone firmly joined together, treasure-house of all wisdom, symbol and promise of the coveted goal for a human race thirsting for knowledge, longing for the final revelation of truth. And since knowledge always means power, too, with every new insight that Man gains into the forces at work in Nature, he always opens up also a new gateway to an ultimate mastery over them, to the possibility of harnessing these natural forces and making them obey his every command.

But this is not all—nor even the most important part of it. Man wants not only knowledge and power. He wants also a standard, a measure of his actions, a criterion of what is valuable and what is worthless. He wants an ideology and philosophy of life, to assure him of the greatest good on earth

* A Lecture delivered by Max Planck in November, 1941.

—peace of mind. And if religion fails to satisfy his longing, he will seek a substitute in exact science. I refer here merely to the endeavors of Monism, founded by outstanding scholars, philosophers and natural scientists, a school of thought which commanded high respect only as recently as a short generation ago.

Yet, in these our days hardly a word is being heard about the Monists, although the structure of their ideology was unquestionably erected to endure for a long time to come, and it started out on its career with high hopes and great promises. There must be something wrong somewhere! And in fact, if we take a closer look and scrutinize the edifice of exact science more intently, we must very soon become aware of the fact that it has a dangerously weak point—namely, its very foundation. Its foundation is not braced, reinforced properly, in every direction, so as to enable it to withstand external strains and stresses. In other words, exact science is not built on any principle of such universal validity, and at the same time of such portentous meaning, as to be fit to support the edifice properly. To be sure, exact science relies everywhere on exact measurements and figures, and is therefore fully entitled to bear its proud name, for the laws of logic and mathematics must undoubtedly be regarded as reliable. But even the keenest logic and the most exact mathematical calculation cannot produce a single fruitful result in the absence of a premise of unerring accuracy. Nothing can be gained from nothing.

No phrase has ever engendered more misunderstanding and confusion in the world of scholars than the expression, *"Science without Presuppositions."* It was coined originally by Theodor Mommsen, and was meant to express that scientific analysis and research must steer clear of every preconceived opinion. But it could not be, nor was it, intended to mean that scientific research needs no presuppositions at all. Scientific thought must link itself to something, and the big question is, *where*. This question has occupied the minds of the most profound thinkers of all epochs and all nations, since time immemorial, from Thales to Hegel, setting in motion all forces of man's imagination and logic. But it has been demonstrated again and again that a final, conclusive answer cannot be found. Perhaps the most impressive proof of this negative finding is that until now all attempts have failed to discover a world view uniformly acceptable, in its general features at least, by all minds capable of judgment. The only conclusion which this fact permits, according to every dictate of reason, is that it is absolutely impossible to place exact science in an *a priori* manner on a universal foundation possessing a fixed and inclusive content.

Thus, at the very outset of our quest for the meaning of exact science, we are confronted by an obstacle which must be a disappointment to everybody who is seriously striving for knowledge. In fact, this obstacle has driven many a critically disposed thinker to join the ranks of the skeptics. And a no less regrettable fact is that there are perhaps just as many, or even more, individuals of the opposite disposition whom the fear of falling victims to skepticism—an ideology which they consider intolerable—drives to look for salvation to prophets of creeds like, for instance, anthroposophy. Such prophets appear on the scene in all epochs, not excepting our own, with their brand new message of salvation, and they often succeed, with an amazing rapidity, in gathering a following of enthusiastic disciples, eventually to make their exit from the stage and to sink back into the all-engulfing abyss of oblivion.

Is there a way out of this fatal dilemma? And where can it be found? This is the first question to claim our attention. I shall attempt to show that there is a positive answer to it, and that this answer will cast a light both on the meaning and limits of exact science. I submit to the judgment of each of you the validity of my proposed resolution of the problem.

I.

If we seek a foundation for the edifice of exact science which is capable of withstanding every criticism, we must first of all tone down our demands considerably. We must not expect to succeed at a stroke, by one single lucky idea, in hitting on an axiom of universal validity, to permit us to develop, with exact methods, a complete scientific structure. We must be satisfied initially to discover some form of truth which no skepticism can attack. In other words, we must set our sights not on what we would like to know, but first on what we do know with certainty.

Now then, among all the facts that we do know and can report to each other, which is the one that is absolutely the most certain, the one that is not open even to the most minute doubt? This question admits of but one answer: "That which we experience with our own body." And since exact science deals with the exploration of the outside world, we may immediately go on to say: "They are the impressions we receive in life from the outside world directly through our sense organs, the eyes, ears, etc." If we see, hear or touch something, it is clearly a given fact which no skeptic can endanger.

To be sure, we speak also of illusions, but never with the intention of implying that the sense perceptions involved are incorrect or even questionable. For instance, when a person happens to be deceived by a mirage, the fault lies not with his perception of the visual image, which is actually present, but in his inferences which draw false conclusions from the given sensory data. The sensory impression is always a given fact, and therefore incontestable. What conclusions the individual attaches to it, is another story, which need not concern us for the time being. Therefore, the content of the sensory impressions is the most suitable and only unassailable foundation on which to build the structure of exact science.

If we call the sum total of sensory impressions *"the sense world,"* we may state briefly that exact science issues from the experienced sense world. The sense world is that which, so to speak, furnishes science with the raw material for its labors.

However, this seems to be a very meager result. For the content of the sense world is, in any case, only something of a subjective character. Every individual has his own senses, and in general, the senses of one individual are quite different from those of another, whereas the aim of exact science is to achieve objective, universally valid knowledge. It may seem, therefore, that in adopting our present approach we have been following the wrong track.

But we must not jump to conclusions. For it will become manifest that considerable progress can be made along the line of advance now open to us. Considered as a whole, the matter reduces itself to the fact that we human beings have no direct access to the knowledge conveyed to us by

exact science, but must acquire it one by one, step
by step, at the cost of painstaking labors of years
and centuries.

Now, if we examine the content of our sense
world, it obviously falls apart into as many separate fields as we have sense organs—there is a
field corresponding to sight, another to hearing,
and still others corresponding to the senses of
touch, smell, taste and heat. These fields are
totally different from each other, and have initially nothing in common. There is no immediate,
direct bridge between the perception of colors
and the perception of sounds. An affinity, such as
may be assumed by many art lovers to exist between a certain shade of color and a certain musical pitch, is not directly given, but is the creation,
stimulated by personal experiences, of our reflective power of imagination.

Since exact science deals with measurable magnitudes, it is concerned primarily with those sensory impressions which admit of quantitative data
—in other words, the world of sight, the world
of hearing, and the world of touch. These fields
supply science with its raw material for study

and research, and science goes to work on it with the tools of a logically, mathematically and philosophically disciplined reasoning.

II.

What, then, is the meaning of this work of science? Briefly put, it consists in the task of introducing order and regularity into the wealth of heterogeneous experiences conveyed by the various fields of the sense world. Under closer examination, this task proves to be fully consistent with the task which we are habitually peforming in our lives ever since our earliest infancy, in order to find our way and place in our environment. This is a task which has kept man busy ever since he first began to think at all in order to be able to hold his own in the struggle for existence. Scientific reasoning does not differ from ordinary everyday thinking in kind, but merely in degree of refinement and accuracy, more or less as the performance of the microscope differs from that of the naked eye. The truth of this statement, and that it must necessarily be so, is evident from the very fact that there is only one kind of logic, and, therefore, even scientific logic cannot deduce anything else from given presuppositions than can the ordinary logic of untrained common sense.

We shall therefore obtain an intuitively clear understanding of the results which science achieves through its labors, if we take our point of departure from the experiences known and familiar to us from daily life. If we review our own personal, individual development, and consider the point which our world view has gradually reached in the course of the years, we can say that we are trying to use the facts of experience as the foundation for a unified, comprehensive and practically serviceable picture of the world in which we live; that we conceive the outside world as filled with objects which act on our various sense organs, thus producing our different sensory impressions.

However, since this practical world picture which every human being carries within himself is not a directly given notion, but an idea elaborated gradually on the basis of facts of experience, it is possessed of no final character. It is changed and adjusted by every new datum of experience, from infancy to adulthood, first at a quicker, then at a slower pace. The same principle applies to the scientific world picture. The scientific world picture or the so-called phenomenological world is also not final and constant, but is in a process of constant change and improvement. It differs from the practical world picture of daily life not in kind, but in its finer structure. It is to the world picture of daily life approximately as the world picture of the adult human being is to the world picture of the human child. Therefore the best start toward a correct understanding of the scientific world picture will be to investigate the most primitive world picture, the naïve world picture of the child.

Let us, therefore, try to place ourselves, as best we can, in the child's mind and world of ideas. As soon as the child begins to think, he begins to form his world picture. For this purpose, he directs his attention toward the impressions which he receives through his sense organs. He tries to classify them, and in this endeavor he makes all kinds of discoveries, such as, for instance, that there is a certain orderly interrelation between the inherently different impressions conveyed by the senses of sight, touch and hearing. If you give the child a toy, let us say, a rattle, he will find that the tactile sensation is always accompanied by a corresponding visual sensation, and as he moves the rattle back and forth, he also perceives a certain regular auditory sensation.

While in this instance the different mutually independent sense worlds appear to be interlocking to a certain degree, on other occasions the child will make an observation which he will find to be no less remarkable—that certain impressions which are completely indistinguishable from one another and have their origin in a common sense world, may nevertheless be of a totally different character. Thus, for instance, the child may look at a round electric light and observe that it looks just like the full moon. The light sensation may be exactly the same. Yet, the child finds a great difference, for he can touch the lamp, but not the moon; he can pass his hand around the lamp, but not around the moon.

What, then, does the child think as he makes these discoveries? First of all, he wonders. This feeling of wonderment is the source and inexhaustible fountain-head of his desire for knowledge. It drives the child irresistibly on to solve the mystery, and if in his attempt he encounters a causal relationship, he will not tire of repeating the same experiment ten times, a hundred times, in order to taste the thrill of discovery over and over again. Thus, by a process of incessant labor from day to day, the child eventually develops his world picture, to the degree needed by him in practical life.

The more the child matures, and the more complete his world picture becomes, the less frequently he finds reason to wonder. And when he has grown up, and his world picture has solidified and taken on a certain form, he accepts this picture as a matter of course and ceases to wonder. Is this because the adult has fully fathomed the correlations and the necessity of the structure of his world picture? Nothing could be more erroneous than this idea. No!—The reason why the adult no longer wonders is not because he has solved the riddle of life, but because he has grown accustomed to the laws governing his world picture. But the problem of why these particular laws and no others hold, remains for him just as amazing and inexplicable as for the child. He who does not comprehend this situation, misconstrues its profound significance, and he who has reached the stage where he no longer wonders about anything, merely demonstrates that he has lost the art of reflective reasoning.

Rightly viewed, the real marvel is that we encounter natural laws at all which are the same for men of all races and nations. This is a fact which is by no means a matter of course. And the subsequent marvel is that for the most part these laws have a scope which could not have been anticipated in advance.

Thus, the element of the wondrous in the structure of the world picture increases with the discovery of every new law. This holds true even of scientific research and inquiry in our own day, which continually produce something new. Just think of the mysteries of the cosmic rays, or the mysterious hormones, or the remarkable revelations of the electron microscope. To the research scientist, no less than to the child, it is always a gratifying experience and an added stimulus to encounter a new wonder, and he will labor industriously to solve the riddle by repeating the same experiments with his refined instruments just as the child does with his primitive rattle.

However, let us not leap too far ahead, but

proceed in an orderly fashion. First, let us investigate in what respect the structure of the child's world differs from the sense world as originally given. The first fact to claim our attention is that sensations, the sole and exclusive constituents of the original world picture, have been driven appreciably into the background. The dominant elements of this world picture are not sensations, but the objects which produce them. The toy is the dominant element, and the tactile, visual and auditory sensations are merely secondary consequences. But we would not do full justice to the state of affairs were we to say simply that this world picture is nothing but a synthesis of different sensory impressions achieved with the help of the unifying concept of *thing.* For, conversely, a single undifferentiated sense experience may correspond to several different objects. An example of this possibility is the previously mentioned case of an illuminated surface which produces in us a definite sensory impression, and yet is sometimes attributed to an electric light while at other times to the full moon. This is a case of a single undifferentiated sensation which corresponds to two different objects. The contrast, therefore, lies deeper, and can be characterized exhaustively only by introducing the concept of an objectively valid regularity. The sensations produced by objects are private, and vary from one individual to another. But the world picture, the world of objects, is the same for all human beings, and we may say that the transition from the sense world to the world picture amounts to a replacement of a disordered subjective manifold by a constant objective order, of chance by law, and of variable appearance by stable substance.

The world of objects, in contrast to the sense world, is therefore called the *real world*. Yet, one must be careful when using the word, *real*. It must be taken here in a qualified sense only. For this word has the connotation of something absolutely stable, permanent, immutable, whereas the objects of the child's world picture could not rightly be claimed to be immutable. The toy is not immutable, it may break or burn. The electric lamp can be smashed to smithereens. This precludes their being called *real* in the sense just mentioned.

This sounds both self-evident and trivial. But we must bear in mind that in the case of the scientific world picture, where as we have seen, the situation is quite analogous, this state of affairs was by no means found to be self-evident. For just as to the child the toy is the true reality, so for decades and centuries the atoms were taken by science to constitute the true reality in natural processes. The atoms were considered to be that which remains immutable when an object is smashed or burned, thus representing permanency in the midst of all change—until one day, to everybody's astonishment, it was found that even atoms could change. Therefore, whenever in the sequel we refer to the "real world," we shall be using the word *real* primarily in a qualified, naive sense, adjusted to the particular character of the dominant world picture, and we must constantly bear in mind that a change in the world picture may go hand in hand, simultaneously, with that which people call "real."

Every world picture is characterized by the real elements, of which it is composed. The real world of exact science, the scientific world picture, evolved from the real world of practical life. But even this world picture is not final, but changes all the time, step by step, with every advance of inquiry.

Such a stage of development is represented by that scientific world picture which today we are accustomed to call "classical." Its real elements, and hence its characteristic feature, were the chemical atoms. In our own day, scientific research, fructified by the theory of relativity and the quantum theory, stands at the threshold of a higher stage of development, ready to mould a new world picture for itself. The real elements of this coming world picture are no longer the chemical atoms, but electrons and protons, whose mutual interactions are governed by the velocity of light and by the elementary quantum of action. From today's point of view, therefore, we must regard the realism of the classical world picture as naïve. But nobody can tell whether some day in the future the same words will not be used in referring to our modern world picture, too.

III.

But what is the meaning of this constant shift in what we call "real"? Is it not utterly unsatisfactory to all men who seek definite scientific insight?

The answer to this question must be, first of all, that our immediate concern is not whether or not the situation is satisfactory, but what its essentials are. But the pursuit of this question will lead to a discovery which we must regard as the greatest of all the wonders previously mentioned. First of all, it must be noted that the continual displacement of one world picture by another is dictated by no human whim or fad, but by an irresistible force. Such a change becomes inevitable whenever scientific inquiry hits upon a new fact in nature for which the currently accepted world picture cannot account. To cite a concrete example, such a fact is the velocity of light in empty space, and another is the part played by the elementary quantum of action in the regular occurrence of all atomic processes. These two facts, and many more, could not be incorporated in the classical world picture, and consequently, the classical world picture had to yield its place to a new world picture.

This in itself is enough to make one wonder. But the circumstance which calls for ever greater wonderment, because it is not self-evidently a matter of course by any means, is that the new world picture does not wipe out the old one, but permits it to stand in its entirety, and merely adds a special condition for it. This special condition involves a certain limitation, but because of this very fact it simplifies the world picture considerably. In fact, the laws of classical mechanics continue to hold satisfactorily for all the processes in which the velocity of light may be considered to be infinitely great, and the quantum of action to be infinitely small. In this way we are able to link up in a general manner mechanics with electro-dynamics, to substitute energy for mass, and moreover, to reduce the building blocks of the universe from the ninety-two different atom types of the classical world picture to two—electrons and protons. Every material body consists of electrons and protons. The combination of a proton and an electron is either a neutron or a hydrogen atom, according as the electron becomes attached to the proton or circles about it. All the physical and chemical properties of a body may be deduced from the type of its structure.

The formerly accepted world picture is thus

preserved, except for the fact that now it takes on the aspect of a special section of a still larger, still more comprehensive, and at the same time still more homogeneous picture. This happens in all cases within our experience. As the multitude of the natural phenomena observed in all fields unfolds in an ever richer and more variegated profusion, the scientific world picture, which is derived from them, assumes an always clearer and more definite form. The continuing changes in the world picture do not therefore signify an erratic oscillation in a zigzag line, but a progress, an improvement, a completion. In establishing this fact I have, in my opinion, indicated the basically most important accomplishment that scientific research can claim.

But what is the direction of this progress, and what is its ultimate goal? The direction, evidently, is the constant improvement of the world picture by reducing the real elements contained in it to a higher reality of a less naïve character. The goal, on the other hand, is the creation of a world picture, with real elements which no longer require an improvement, and therefore represent the ultimate reality. A demonstrable attainment of this goal will—or can—never be ours. But in order to have at least a name for it, for the time being, we call the ultimate reality "the real world," in the absolute, metaphysical sense of the word, *real*. This is to be construed as expressing the fact that the *real* world—in other words, objective nature —stands behind everything explorable. In contrast to it, the scientific world picture gained by experience—the *phenomenological world*—remains always a mere approximation, a more or less well divined model. As there is a material object behind every sensation, so there is a metaphysical reality behind everything that human experience shows to be real. Many philosophers object to the word, *"behind."* They say: "Since in exact science all concepts and all measures are reducible to sensations, in the last analysis the meaning of every scientific finding also refers only to the sense world, and it is inadmissible, or at least superfluous, to postulate the existence behind this world of a metaphysical world, totally inaccessible to direct scientific inquiry and examination." The only proper reply to this argument is, simply, that in the above sentence the word, *behind,* must not be interpreted in an external or spatial sense. Instead of "behind," we could just as well say, *"in"* or *"within."* Metaphysical reality does not stand spatially *behind* what is given in experience, but lies fully *within* it. "Nature is neither core nor shell—she is everything at once." The essential point is that the world of sensation is not the only world which may conceivably exist, but that there is still another world. To be sure, this other world is not directly accessible to us, but its existence is indicated, time and again, with compelling clarity, not only by practical life, but also by the labors of science. For the great marvel of the scientific world picture, becoming progressively more complete and perfect, necessarily impels the investigator to seek its ultimate form. And since one must assume the existence of that which one seeks, the scientist's assumption of the actual existence of a "real world," in the absolute sense of the word, eventually grows into a firm conviction which nothing can shake any more. This firm belief in the absolute *Real* in nature is what constitutes for him the given, self-evident premise of his work; it fortifies repeatedly his hope of eventually groping his way still a little nearer to the essence of objective Nature, and of thereby gaining further clues to her secrets.

Since the real world, in the absolute sense of the word, is independent of individual personalities, and in fact of all human intelligence, every discovery made by any individual acquires a completely universal significance. This gives the inquirer, wrestling with his problem in quiet seclusion, the assurance that every discovery will win the unhesitating recognition of all experts throughout the entire world, and in this feeling of the importance of his work lies his happiness. It compensates him fully for many a sacrifice which he must make in his daily life.

The sublime nature of such a goal must, necessarily, dwarf into insignificance any doubt engendered by the difficulties encountered while shaping the scientific world picture. It is particularly important to emphasize this in our own day, for nowadays such difficulties are sometimes regarded as serious impediments to the salutary progress of scientific work. It is an odd fact that experimental difficulties are so regarded to a lesser degree than theoretical ones. The circumstance that with the increasing demands on the accuracy of measurements the instruments, too, become more intricate, is understood and accepted as a matter of course. But the fact that in the endeavor to improve continually the expansion of systematic interrelations, it is necessary to use definitions and concepts which diverge more and more from traditional forms and intuitive notions, is sometimes cited as a reproach against theoretical research, and is even viewed as indicating that theoretical research is entirely on the wrong track.

Nothing could be more shortsighted than such a view. For if we stop to think that the improvement of the world picture goes hand in hand with an approach to the metaphysically "real world," the expectation that the definitions and concepts of the objectively real world picture will not diverge too much from the framework created by the classical world picture, amounts basically to a demand that the metaphysically real world be completely intelligible in terms of ideas derived from the former naive world picture. This is a demand that can be never fulfilled. We simply cannot expect to recognize and discern the finer structure of something, so long as we flatly refuse to view it otherwise than with the naked eye. Yet, in this respect there is no reason for fear. The development of the scientific world picture is a matter of absolute necessity. The experiences gained with the refined instruments of measurement demand inexorably that certain firmly-rooted intuitive notions be abandoned and replaced by new, more abstract conceptual structures, for which the appropriate intuitions are still to be found and developed. Thus, they are the landmarks to guide theoretical research on its road from the naive concept of reality to the metaphysical "Real."

But significant as the achievements may be, and near as the desired goal may seem, there always remains a gaping chasm, unbridgeable from the point of view of exact science, between the real world of phenomenology and the real world of metaphysics. This chasm is the source of a constant tension, which can never be balanced, and which is the inexhaustible source of the insatiable thirst for knowledge within the true research scientist. But at the same time, we catch here a glimpse of the boundaries which exact science is unable to cross. May its results be ever so deep and far-reaching, it can never succeed in taking the last step which would take it into the realm of metaphysics. The fact that although we feel inevitably compelled to postulate the existence of a *real world,* in the absolute sense, we can never fully comprehend its nature, constitutes the irrational element which exact science can never shake off, and the proud name, "Exact Science," must not be permitted to cause anybody to underestimate the significance of this element of irrationality. On the other hand, the very fact that science sets its own limits on the basis of scientific knowledge itself, appears well suited to strengthen everybody's confidence in the reliability of that knowledge, knowledge obtained on the basis of incontestable presupposition and with the help of rigorous experimental and theoretical methods.

If now, we cast our glance, from the viewpoint now established, back on the starting point of our considerations, and on the entire train of thoughts pursued, the results gained will become even clearer. We began our deliberations with a definite disillusionment. We sought a universal foundation on which to erect the edifice of exact science, a foundation of indisputable firmness and security— and we failed to find it. Now in the light of the insights gained, we recognize that our quest was doomed to failure even before it started. For, basically considered, our attempt was based on the idea of starting out on our scientific exploration from something irrevocably real, whereas we have now come to understand that such ultimate reality is of a metaphysical character and can never be completely known. This is the intrinsic reason which doomed to failure every previous attempt to erect the edifice of exact science on a universal foundation valid *a priori*. We had to be satisfied, instead, with a starting point which was of inviolable solidity and yet of an extremely limited significance, since it was based solely on individual data of experience. It is at this modest point that scientific research enters with its exact methods, and it works its way step by step from the specific to the always more general. To this end, it must set and continually keep its sights on the objective reality which it seeks, and in this sense exact science can never dispense with *Reality* in the metaphysical sense of the term. But the real world of metaphysics is not the starting point, but the goal of all scientific endeavor, a beacon winking and showing the way from an inaccesibly remote distance.

The assurance that every new discovery, and every new fact of knowledge gained from it, will bring us nearer to the goal, must compensate us for the numerous, and certainly not negligible, drawbacks which are necessarily created by the continual abatement of the intuitive character and ease of application of the world picture. In fact, the present scientific world picture, as against the original naïve world picture, shows an odd, almost alien aspect. The immediately experienced sense impressions, the primordial sources of scientific activity, have dropped totally out of the world picture, in which sight, hearing and touch no longer play a part. A glance into a modern scientific laboratory shows that the functions of these senses have been taken over by a collection of extremely complex, intricate and specialized apparatus, contrived and constructed for handling problems which can be formulated only with the aid of abstract concepts, mathematical and geometric symbols, and which often are beyond the layman's power of understanding. One might feel completely at sea trying to puzzle out the meaning of exact science, and exact science has even been accused on this account of having lost its firm footing with the loss of its original intuitive character. But he who persists in this opinion, despite the reasons cited, is beyond help, and will be as unable to make any essential contribution to the progress of exact science as an experimenter who insists, as a matter of principle, on working always with primitive instruments only. For exact science demands more than a gift of intuition and willingness to work hard. It demands also very involved, painstaking, tedious attention to details, for which many scientists must often pool their efforts in order to prepare their branch of science for the next step on the ladder of gradual progress. To be sure, when the pioneer in science sends forth the groping feelers of his thoughts, he must have a vivid intuitive imagination, for new ideas are not generated by deduction, but by an artistically creative imagination. Nevertheless, the worth of a new idea is invariably determined, not by the degree of its intuitiveness—which, incidentally, is to a major extent a matter of experience and habit—but by the scope and accuracy of the individual laws to the discovery of which it eventually leads.

Of course, every step forward means also that the difficulty of the task increases, the demands on the analyst grow more exacting, and the need for an expedient division of labor becomes always more urgently imperative. In particular, the division of science into experimental and theoretical was completed about a century ago. Experimenters are the shocktroops of science. They perform the decisive experiments, carry out the all-important work of measurement. An experiment is a question which science poses to Nature, and a measurement is the recording of Nature's answer. But before an experiment can be performed, it must be planned—the question to Nature must be formulated before being posed. Before the result of a measurement can be used, it must be interpreted—Nature's answer must be understood properly. These two tasks are those of the theorist, who finds himself always more and more dependent on the tools of abstract mathematics. Of course, this does not mean that the experimenter does not also engage in theoretical deliberations. The foremost classical example of a major achievement produced by such a division of labor is the creation of spectrum analysis by the joint efforts of Robert Bunsen, the experimenter, and Gustav Kirchhoff, the theorist. Since then, spectrum analysis has been continually developing and bearing ever richer fruit.

Whenever an experimental finding contradicts the accepted theory, another step on the ladder of progress is thereby announced, for the contradiction signifies that the accepted theory must be overhauled and improved. But the question as to just where and how to change it, entails serious difficulties. For the more tried an existing theory is, the more sensitive it is, and the stronger resistance it puts up to every attempt to alter it. In this respect, it behaves like a highly complex, widely ramified organism, whose individual component parts are mutually interdependent and are so closely interlinked that a reaction to any stimulus at any one point is also manifested automatically at quite different and, seemingly, very remote places. This gives rise to new questions, which can be investigated experimentally, and thus it may lead to consequences, the bearing and importance of which no one could suspect at the outset. This is how the theory of relativity was born, and this is the story behind the genesis of the quantum theory. In our own days, the constant growth and advancement of the youngest branch of natural science, nuclear physics, brought about and implemented by a reciprocal supplementation of experiment and theory, is another typical example of such fruitful collaboration.

IV.

But why all this enormous labor, demanding the best efforts of countless soldiers of science during their entire lives? Is the ultimate result—which, as we have seen, in its individual details always drifts away from the immediately given facts of life—truly worth this costly effort?

These questions would indeed be justified if the meaning of exact science were limited to a certain gratification of man's instinctive yearning for knowledge and insight. But its significance goes considerably deeper. The roots of exact science feed in the soil of human life. But its link to it is twofold. For it not only has its source in experience, but also has a retroactive effect on human life, both material and spiritual, and the more freely it can unfold itself, the stronger and more fruitful is this effect. This manifests itself in a very peculiar manner. First, as we have found, when science works on the world picture of its own making, its quest of metaphysical Reality causes it to drift always farther and farther away from the immediate facts and interests of life, since it always takes to less intuitive and more solitary trails. But these trails, and only these, are the very paths leading toward a discernment of new laws of interrelations, which would be inaccessible in any other way, and which can then be made relevant for human experience and thus made to serve human needs.

This fact can be observed in countless individual instances. Here, too, a far-reaching division of labor has proved its worth excellently. The first step, the moulding of the world picture from its beginnings in ordinary experience, is the task of pure science. The second step, the practical utilization of the scientific world picture, is the task of technology. Both these tasks are equally important, and since either of them demands a man's full energy, if an individual scientist wants to make progress in his work, he must concentrate all his energy on one single task and for the time being forget completely other problems and interests. For this reason, never reproach the scholar too harshly for his other-worldliness and his indifference to important problems of human society. Without such a one-sided attitude, Heinrich Hertz could never have discovered radio waves, or Robert Koch the tubercle bacillus. These gifts of pure scientific research to practical life have their counterparts in the manifold stimuli and intelligent assistance which science receives from technology, a fact that is becoming progressively more manifest in our day and whose importance cannot be assessed too highly.

I feel I must discuss here a little more closely, by way of an example, a very recent and very impressive case of the often quite unsuspected close interrelation of science and technology. For a great number of years, only men of pure science were interested in the distinctive facts of atomic transformations. To be sure, the magnitude of the energies thus released did attract attention, yet since atoms were so infinitesimally small, no serious thought was given to the possibility that one day they might acquire practical significance, too. Today, due to new findings in the field of artificial radioactivity, this question has taken an astonishing turn. The investigations of Otto Hahn and his collaborators have established the fact that a uranium atom bombarded by a neutron splits into several parts. Two or three neutrons are liberated, and each of them continues on its own path and may, in its turn, collide with a uranium atom and split it. Thus the effects may multiply; and it may happen that as a consequence of the increasing bombardment of uranium atoms by the liberated neutrons the energy thus released will swell like an avalanche within a very short time. To visualize this, think of the well known example of chain letters. With the number of available atoms, this chain reaction may reach quite enormous, hardly conceivable proportions. Of course, an indispensable prerequisite for this effect is that the free neutrons, prior to their hitting uranium nuclei, are not captured by other atoms and are thus either permanently absorbed by the latter or deflected away from uranium nuclei.

A specific computation has shown that the

amount of energy released in this manner in a cubic meter (35.314 cubic feet) of powdered uranium oxide within one one-hundredth of second is sufficient to lift a weight of 1,000,000,000 metric tons to a height of almost 17 miles. This amount of energy could replace the output of all the big power plants of the world combined for many years.

Up to quite recently, a technical utilization of the energy latent in the nuclei of atoms might have appeared as a utopian dream. But it was made a reality about 1942, by the impressive collaboration of British and American scientists with American industry, backed by huge government subsidies. At the present moment, several "uranium piles" are operating in America, and the heat continually produced by them is sufficient to raise the temperature of the Victoria River in the state of Washington by 1 degree Centigrade. So far as the reports disclose, these vast amounts of energy are still unused. Right now, the problem is to get rid of them in a harmless way. But these same piles furnish also the raw materials for the atomic bombs, in which vast amounts of the nuclear energy of the atom are liberated within a fraction of a second, producing explosions beside which the devastation caused by all chemical explosives fades into insignificance. No words can be strong enough to over-emphasize the danger of self-extermination which threatens the entire human race, should a future war bring about the use of a large number of such bombs. Human imagination is incapable of conceiving the possible consequences. A particularly eloquent and forceful plea for peace is the memory of the 80,000 dead of Hiroshima and the 40,000 dead of Nagasaki, a plea addressed to all nations, and especially to their responsible leaders.

In view of these facts, perhaps many who have lost the art of wondering may feel disposed to learn it anew. And in fact, compared with immeasurably rich, ever young Nature, advanced as man may be in scientific knowledge and insight, he must forever remain the wondering child and must constantly be prepared for new surprises.

Thus we see ourselves governed all through life by a higher power, whose nature we shall never be able to define from the viewpoint of exact science. Yet, no one who thinks can ignore it. A thinking human being, who has not only scientific but also metaphysical interests, must choose one of two possible attitudes: Either fear and hostile resistance or reverence and trusting devotion. If we reflect on all the unspeakable suffering and incessant destruction of life and property which have plagued mankind since time immemorial, we may be tempted to agree with the pessimistic philosophers who consider life worthless and deny the possibility of permanent progress, of a betterment of mankind, and who profess instead that it is the fate of every human civilization to turn blindly against itself as soon as it has reached a certain peak, and to destroy itself without sense or purpose.

May exact science be cited as an evidence of such a far-reaching view? The answer must be "No," if for no other reason, because science is not qualified to decide the question. From the scientific point of view, one might just as well, and perhaps with even more justification, endorse the opposite opinion. It would require merely an extension of the range of observation, a thinking not in terms of centuries but of many millennia. Or is there anybody who would seriously deny that during the past one hundred thousand years *homo sapiens* has made progress and has improved himself? Why should this progress not continue further—if not in a straight line, then at least in waves?

Of course, such considerations, such a long-range view, are no help to the individual. They cannot bring him succor in his hour of need or cure his pain. The individual has no alternative but to fight bravely in the battle of life, and to bow in silent surrender to the will of a higher power which rules over him. For no man is born with a legal claim to happiness, success and prosperity in life. We must therefore accept every favorable decision of Providence, each single hour of happiness, as an unearned gift, one that imposes an obligation. The only thing that we may claim for our own with absolute assurance, the greatest good that no power in the world can take from us, and one that can give us more permanent happiness than anything else, is integrity of soul, which manifests itself in a conscientious performance of one's duty. And he whom good fortune has permitted to co-operate in the erection of the edifice of exact science, will find his satisfaction and inner happiness, with our great poet Goethe, in the knowledge that he has explored the explorable and quietly venerates the inexplorable.

The Concept of Causality in Physics

In the fight currently raging about the meaning and validity of the Law of Causality in modern physics, every attempt to clarify the conflicting opinions must begin with the statement that in this connection everything depends on a clear understanding of the sense in which the word "causality" is used in the science of physics. To be sure, it is agreed *a priori* that whenever a reference is made to a "causal relationship" between two successive events or occurrences, this term is understood to designate a certain regular connection between them, calling the earlier one the *cause,* and the latter one the *effect.* But the question is: What constitutes this specific type of connection? Is there any infallible sign to indicate that a happening in nature is causally determined by another?

It follows from the numerous inquiries heretofore undertaken into this question that the best and safest way to approach a clear answer is to relate the question to the possibility of making accurate predictions. In fact, there can be no more incontestable way to prove the causal relationship between any two events than to demonstrate that from the occurrence of one it is always possible to infer in advance the occurrence of the other. This point was quite familiar to the farmer who gave a visual demonstration to some sceptical peasants of the causal relationship between artificial fertilizers and the fertility of the soil, by intensively fertilizating his clover fields in certain narrow strips having the form of letters, so as to make the following sentence appear: "This strip was fertilized with calcium sulfate."

Therefore, I want to base all our subsequent considerations on the following simple proposition, equally applicable outside of the realm of physics: *"An occurrence is causally determined if it can be predicted with certainty."* Of course, this sentence is meant to express only that the possibility of making an accurate prediction for the future constitutes an infallible criterion of the presence of a causal relationship, but not that it is synonymous with the latter. I need to mention merely the well known example that we can pre-

dict with a certainty while it is still day the coming of night, and yet this does not make day the
cause of night.

But conversely, it also often happens that we
assume the presence of a causal relationship even
in cases where there is no question at all of the
possibility of making accurate predictions. Just
think of weather forecasts. The unreliability of
weather prophets has become proverbial, and yet
there is hardly any trained meteorologist who
does not consider the atmospheric processes to be
causally determined. All these considerations indicate that in order to find the right clues to the
concept of causality, we must go still a little
deeper.

In the case of weather forecasts, the thought
suggests itself that their unreliability is due merely
to the size and complicated nature of the object of
the analysis, i.e. the atmosphere. If we single out
a small portion of it—for instance, a cubic foot of
air—we will be far more likely to make accurate
predictions about its reaction to external influences, such as compression, heat, moisture, etc.
We are familiar with certain laws of physics
which enable us to predict, with more or less cer-

tainty, the readings of the corresponding measurements, such as the increase in pressure, rise in
temperature, condensation, etc.

However, if we observe things still a little more
closely, we shall soon reach a very remarkable
conclusion. Simple as we may make the conditions, and precise as our measuring instruments
may be, we shall never succeed in calculating in
advance the results of the actual measurements
with an absolute accuracy, in other words in making the predicted value of a magnitude agree to
the last decimal place with the figure actually
registered by the instruments; there always remains a certain margin of uncertainty—in contrast to the calculations in pure mathematics, as
in the case of the square root of 2 or of π, which
can be given accurately to any number of decimal
places. And whatever applies to mechanical and
thermal processes, holds true for all fields of
physics, including electricity and optics.

Thus, all the above cited experiences force us
to recognize the following principle as a firmly
established fact: *It is never possible to predict a
physical occurrence with unlimited precision.* If

we now compare this principle with the proposition accepted above as our starting point, namely that an occurrence is causally determined if it can be predicted with certainty, we find ourselves facing an unavoidable dilemma: We may elect *either* to adhere literally to the exact wording of our basic proposition, in which case there cannot exist even one single instance in nature where a causal relationship would have to be assumed to prevail—*or* to subject that basic proposition to a certain modification, so designed as to provide room for the presupposition of strict causality.

A number of contemporary physicists and philosophers have chosen the first alternative. I shall refer to them here as *indeterminists*. They claim that genuine causality, strict regularity, actually does not exist in nature but is merely an illusion created by the operation of certain rules which are never of an exact universal validity, even though they often come very near to it. Upon closer consideration, the indeterminist discovers a statistical root in every law of physics, including the law of gravity and of electrical attraction; he regards them, one and all, as laws of probability,

relating only to mean values of many similar ob-
servations, possessing only an approximate validity for individual instances.

A good example of such a statistical law is the
dependence of the magnitude of gas pressure on
the density and temperature. The pressure of a
gas is produced by the continual impact against
the walls of the vessel of a vast number of gas molecules moving at random in all directions with
great velocity. A summary computation of the
aggregate dynamic effect of their impact reveals
that the pressure against the walls of the vessel is
almost proportional to the density of the gas as
well as to the mean square of the molecular velocity, a result which is in satisfactory agreement
with measurement if we regard the temperature
as a measure of molecular velocity.

A direct confirmation of this theory of gas
pressure is furnished by investigations on the temporal variations of the pressure against a very
small portion of the wall of the vessel. Such variations, produced by random molecular impacts,
can be observed wherever molecules in rapid
flight come in contact with easily movable bodies;
they manifest themselves also in the Brownian

molecular movement, as well as in the fact that very sensitive scales never come to a complete rest, but constantly execute minute irregular vibrations about their position of equilibrium.

Analogously with the gas laws, the indeterminists attribute every other kind of physical regularity, ultimately to the operation of chance. They see nature ruled exclusively by statistics, and their aim is to base all physics on the calculus of probabilities.

Actually, physical science has developed up to now on the very opposite foundation. It chose the *second* one of the two alternatives mentioned above: In order to be able to maintain the full and absolute validity of the law of causality, it modified slightly the basic proposition, that an occurrence is causally determined if it can be predicted with a certainty. This was done by using the word "occurrence" in a somewhat modified sense. Thus, theoretical physics considers as an occurrence not an actual individual process of measurement—which always includes accidental and unessential elements, too—but a certain, merely theoretical process; and in this manner it replaces the sense world, as given to us directly by our sense organs (or alternatively, by the measuring instruments which serve us as sharpened sense organs), by another world, the world picture of physics, which is a conceptual structure, arbitrary to a certain degree, created for the purpose of getting away from the uncertainty involved in every individual measurement and for making possible a precise interrelation of concepts.

Consequently, every measurable physical magnitude, every length, every time interval, every mass, every charge, has a double meaning, according as we regard it as directly given by some measurement, or conceive of it as translated into the world picture of physics. In the first interpretation, it is never capable of a sharp definition, and can therefore never be represented by a quite definite number; but in the world picture of physics it stands for a certain mathematical symbol, which lends itself to manipulation according to quite definite, precise rules. This goes for the height of a tower just as for the duration of the swing of a pendulum or for the brightness of an incandescent lamp. A clear and consistent distinction between the magnitudes of the sense world and the corresponding magnitudes of the world picture is absolutely essential for the clarification of concepts; without such a distinction it is impossible to discuss these questions intelligently and objectively.

It is absolutely untrue, although it is often asserted, that the world picture of physics contains, or may contain, directly observable magnitudes only. On the contrary, directly observable magnitudes are not found at all in the world picture. It contains symbols only. In fact, the world picture even contains constituents which have only a very indirect significance for the sense world, or no significance at all, such as ether waves, partial vibrations, frames of reference, etc. Primarily, such constituents play the part of dead weight or ballast, but they are incorporated because of the decisive advantage assured by the introduction of the world picture—that it permits us to carry through a strict determinism.

Of course, the world picture always remains a mere auxiliary concept. It is self-evident that in the last analysis, the things that really matter, are the occurrences in the sense world and the greatest possible accuracy in predicting them. In classical physics this is achieved as follows: First, an object found in the sense world—for instance, a system of material points—is symbolically represented in some measured condition, i.e. is translated into the world picture. One thus obtains a certain physical structure in a certain initial state. Similarly, suitable symbols are substituted in the framework of the world picture for external influences which operate subsequently on the object. One thus obtains the external forces acting on the structure, and the corresponding boundary conditions. The behavior of the structure is then unambiguously determined for all times by these data, and it can be computed with absolute accuracy from the differential equations of the theory. The coordinates and momenta of all material points of the structure are thus exhibited as quite definite functions of time. If then at any later time the symbols used in the world picture are retranslated into the sense world, one thus obtains a connection between a later occurrence in the sense world and a previous occurrence in the sense world, and this connection can be utilized for an approximate prediction of the later occurrence.

In summary, we may say: While in the sense

world the prediction of an occurrence is always associated with a certain element of uncertainty, in the world picture of physics all occurrences follow one another in accordance with precisely definable laws—they are strictly determined causally. Therefore, the introduction of the world picture of physics—and herein lies its significance— reduces the uncertainty of predicting an occurrence in the sense world to the uncertainty in translating that occurrence from the sense world into the world picture and in retranslating it from the world picture into the sense world.

Classical physics was but little concerned with this uncertainty; its main concern was to follow through the causal point of view in the consideration of the occurrences in the world picture, and this was where it achieved its great results. Specifically, it succeeded also in finding a satisfactory interpretation, on the basis of a strict causality, for the above mentioned irregular vibratory phenomena corresponding to the Brownian molecular movement. The indeterminists see no real problem here. For since they look for irregularity behind every rule, statistical regularity is that which gives them direct satisfaction. Therefore,

they are satisfied also with the assumption that
the collision of two individual molecules, as well
as the impact of the molecules against the wall of
the vessel, occurs solely according to statistical
laws. Nevertheless, this assumption is as little
justified as would be the conclusion that the
charge of an individual electron is located on its
surface just because in a charged conductor the
electrons are all located on its surface. On the
other hand, the determinists who, on the contrary,
look for a rule behind every irregularity, were led
to the problem of basing a theory of the gas laws on
the premise that the collision of two individual
molecules is determined in a strict causal manner.
The solution of this problem was the life work of
Ludwig Boltzmann, and it represents one of the
most beautiful triumphs of theoretic research.
For it not only yields the principle, confirmed by
actual measurements, that the mean energy of the
oscillations about the state of equilibrium is proportional to the absolute temperature, but it permits also a remarkably accurate computation of
the absolute number and mass of the molecules,
based on a measurement of these oscillations, as in
the case of a highly sensitive torsion balance.

Such outstanding achievements seemed to justify the hope that the world picture of classical physics would in principle accomplish its task, and that a steady improvement and refinement of the technique and methods of measurement would progressively reduce the significance of the uncertainties accompanying the translation into and from the sense world. But the introduction of the elementary quantum of action destroyed this hope at one blow and for good.

The so-called Uncertainty Principle, discovered and formulated by Heisenberg, constitutes a characteristic feature of quantum mechanics; it asserts that for any two canonically conjugate magnitudes, such as position and momentum or time and energy, only one can be measured to any desired degree of accuracy, so that an increase in the precision of the measurement of one magnitude is accompanied by a proportional decrease in the precision of measurement of the other. Consequently, when one magnitude is ascertained with absolute accuracy, the other one remains absolutely indefinite.

It is evident that this principle fundamentally precludes the possibility of translating into the sense world, with an arbitrary degree of accuracy, the simultaneous values of the coordinates and momenta of material points, as these are conceived in the world picture of classical physics; this circumstance constitutes a difficulty with respect to the recognition of a universal validity of the principle of strict causality, and it has even caused some indeterminists to regard the law of causality in physics as decisively refuted. However, upon closer scrutiny, this conclusion—founded on a confusion of the world picture with the sense world—proves a rash one, to say the very least. For there is another, more logical way out of the difficulty, a way which has often rendered excellent services on previous occasions—namely, the assumption that the attempt to determine simultaneously both the coordinates and the momentum of a material point is physically completely meaningless. However, the impossibility of giving an answer to a meaningless question must, of course, not be charged up against the law of causality, but solely against the premises which produced that particular question; in other words, in this particular instance, against the assumed structure of the world picture of physics. And since the classical world picture has failed, another must take its place.

This is what actually has happened. The new world picture of quantum mechanics is a product of the need to find a way of reconciling the quantum of action with the principle of strict determinism. For this purpose, the traditional primary constituent of the world picture, the material point, had to be deprived of its basic, elementary character; it was resolved into a system of material waves. These material waves constitute the primary elements of the new world picture. The material point in its old meaning now appears merely as a special borderline case, as an infinitesimally small parcel of waves, the momentum of which is totally indefinite, since its position is definite, according to Heisenberg's uncertainty principle. If we assign a certain range to the position of the material point, the value of the momentum also becomes approximately definite and the laws of classical mechanics then are approximately valid for positions and momenta.

In general, the laws of material waves are basically different from those of the classical mechanics of material points. However, the point of

central importance is that the function charac-
terising material waves, i.e. the wave function or
probability function (the term itself is of no importance here), is fully determined for all places
and times by the initial and boundary conditions,
according to quite definite principles of computation, whether we use Schroedinger's operators,
Heisenberg's matrices, or Dirac's q-numbers.

We thus see that the principle of determinism
is as strictly valid in the world picture of quantum mechanics as in that of classical physics. The
difference consists only in the symbols used and
in the mathematics applied. Accordingly, in the
realm of quantum mechanics, just as formerly in
classical physics, the uncertainty in the prediction
of the occurrences of the sense world is reduced to
an uncertainty in the correlation of world picture
and sense world, in other words, to an uncertainty
in the translation of the symbols of the world picture into the sense world, and *vice versa*. The fact
that this double uncertainty is involved is the
most impressive proof of the importance of re-
taining the principle of determinism within the
world picture.

Nevertheless, even a cursory glance shows how

far the world picture of quantum mechanics has shifted from the sense world, and how much more difficult it is to translate an occurrence from the world picture of quantum mechanics into the sense world or *vice versa*, than was the case in classical physics. In the latter, the meaning of every symbol was immediately and directly intelligible; the position, the velocity, the momentum, the energy of a material point could be determined more or less accurately by measurements, and there appeared no obvious reason to doubt that a steady improvement of the technique and methods of measurement could not eventually reduce the remaining factor of uncertainty below any desired margin. On the other hand, the wave function of quantum mechanics supplies no direct clue whatever for any obvious interpretation of the sense world, simply because it does not refer to ordinary space at all but rather to the configurational space which has as many dimensions as there are coordinates present in the physical structure under consideration. Moreover—and this is where the real trouble lies—the wave function does not give us the values of the coordinates as functions of the time, but merely the probability that the coordinates may possess certain specific values at some specified time.

The indeterminists again seized on this circumstance as the occasion for a new attack against the law of causality. And this time their attack actually seems to promise them success; for on the basis of measurements it is possible to assign merely a statistical significance to the wave function. Nonetheless, once more the defenders of strict causality have the same way out as before: The assumption that the question concerning the meaning of a certain symbol of the world picture of quantum mechanics, such as a material wave, has no definite sense unless one also specifies the condition of the particular measuring apparatus used for translating the symbol into the sense world. For this reason, one is led to talk about the causal effect of the measuring instrument that is employed; and one is thereby expressing the fact that the particular uncertainty in question is determined at least in part by the circumstance that the magnitude of the value to be measured is dependent in a certain regular manner on the method used for measuring it.

However, this auxiliary hypothesis shunts the

entire question to a track, the further course of which is still hidden in darkness. For now the indeterminists are justified in raising the question whether the concept of a causal influence of the measuring instrument on the measuring process has any intelligible meaning, since every attempt to examine such a causal effect directly requires some kind of measurement, and since with every new measurement a new causal influence and therefore a new uncertainty would be introduced into the problem.

And yet, this objection still does not dispose of the matter. For as every experimental physicist knows, besides the direct methods of investigation there exist also indirect ones, and the latter accomplish good results in many a case where the former have failed. However, I must take exception to the view (a very popular one these days, and certainly a very plausible one on the face of it) that a problem in physics merits examination only if it is established in advance that a definite answer to it can be obtained. If physicists had always been guided by this principle, the famous experiment of Michelson and Morley undertaken to measure the so-called absolute velocity of the earth, would never have taken place, and the theory of relativity might still be nonexistent. Accordingly, if the study of a question now regarded fairly universally as meaningless, such as that of the absolute velocity of the earth, has turned out to produce such extraordinary benefits to science, how much more worth while must it be to follow up a problem, the deeper meaning of which is still under debate and which is capable more than any other of enriching research.

But how are we to come to a decision? Obviously, there is no other alternative than to consider the two opposing views, to side with the one that appeals to us more, and then to investigate whether it leads to valuable or to worthless conclusions. At any rate, one must welcome the fact that physicists who are closely interested in this subject are split into two factions; one leans toward the theory of determinism, the other toward indeterminism. So far as I can see, the latter represent the majority nowadays, although it is difficult to establish the facts which may easily change in the course of time. Between these two viewpoints there is also room for a third position which in a certain sense is a mediating one, in that it assigns to certain concepts, such as the force of electrical attraction, a direct significance and a strict uniformity with respect to the sense world; whereas to other concepts, such as material waves, it assigns merely a statistical significance. However, because it lacks systematic unity this view does not appear to be very satisfactory. For this reason, I propose to disregard it now and to confine myself to a somewhat closer analysis of the two fully consistent viewpoints.

The indeterminist is satisfied in his quest for knowledge by the discovery that the wave function of quantum mechanics is merely a probability value. He has no further problem in connection with it. On the other hand, he sees unsolved problems in certain determinate laws of nature, such as Coulomb's law of electrical attraction; for he cannot be satisfied with Coulomb's formula for the force or the potential, but continues to search for exceptions, and is not content until he succeeds in determining the magnitude of the probability that the electrical force differs from Coulomb's value by some arbitrary pre-assigned value.

The determinist thinks along the very opposite lines in all these points. He assigns to Coulomb's law the satisfactory character of absolute validity. On the other hand, he recognizes the wave function as a mere probability magnitude only so long as the measuring instrument used in the study of the wave is disregarded, and he looks for inflexible laws connecting the properties of the wave function and the occurrences in the measuring apparatus. For this purpose, he must obviously include in the subject matter of his investigation both the wave function and the measuring instruments. In other words, he must translate into his physical world picture not only the entire experimental setup used for the production of the material waves—such as the high voltage battery, the incandescent filament, the radioactive compound—but also the measuring apparatus, such as the photographic plate, the ionization chamber, the point counter, together with all the processes occurring therein, and he must deal with all these objects as one single structure, as an isolated system. But this does not yet take care of the problem. On the contrary—it makes it even more complicated. For in this case, if the total structure is to retain its unique character, it must neither be split up nor exposed to external influences, so that a direct examination is completely impossible. Nevertheless it now becomes possible to formulate certain new hypotheses concerning the internal processes of the system, and subsequently to test their consignments. Whether this procedure leads to any actual advance, is a question which only the future can answer. For the time being, it is still impossible to determine clearly what direction will lead to progress. At any rate, all the circumstances mentioned prove that the elementary quantum of action erects an objective barrier which limits the efficiency of the measuring apparatus available to physical science, and that, therefore, the desired progress will only give this barrier even sharper outlines than it had before.

Properly speaking, we have thus reached the end of our considerations which have demonstrated that an adherence to a strictly causal outlook—always taking the word "causal" in the modified sense explained previously—is by no means excluded from the viewpoint of even modern physics, though its necessity can never be proved either *a priori* or *a posteriori*. Nevertheless, not even a convinced determinist—indeed, especially not a convinced determinist—can escape at this point some doubts which prevent him from accepting as fully satisfactory, the interpretation of causality indicated above. For even if it should prove to be feasible to develop further the concept of causality along the lines described, the concept as here proposed involved a serious flaw. For it could be maintained that a relation possessing such profound significance as the causal connection between two successive events represents ought to be independent by its very nature from the human intellect which is considering it. Instead, we have not only linked at the very outset the concept of causality to the human intellect, specifically to the ability of man to predict an occurrence; but we have been able to carry through the deterministic viewpoint only with the expedient of replacing the directly given sense world by the world picture of physics, that is, by a provisional and alterable creation of the human power of imagination. These are anthropomorphic traits which ill-befit fundamental concepts of physics; and the question therefore arises whether it is not possible to give the concept of causality a deeper meaning by divesting it as far as it can be of its anthropomorphic character, and to make it independent of human artifacts such as the world picture of physics. Of course, we shall have to adhere to our basic premise, that an occurrence is causally determined if it can be predicted with a certainty, for otherwise we would lose the only solid foundation for our discussion. And we must feel bound to no less a degree to our second principle, that it is never possible, to predict an occurrence with absolute precision. It accordingly follows that if we are to speak at all of causality in nature, we must introduce some modification into our first basic proposition. To this extent the situation remains as it was before. But the type of modification which we introduced previously into the first basic proposition can be replaced by a totally different one.

In the preceding discussion what was modified was the object of the prediction—the occurrence. For we related the occurrences not to the directly given sense world, but to an artificially created world picture, and we thus found it possible to determine occurrences accurately. But instead of modifying the object of predictions we can alter our notion of the subject of the prediction, that is, of the predicting intellect. For every prediction presupposes somebody who does the predicting. Therefore, in the following discussion we shall direct our attention solely to the predicting subject, and shall consider as the objects of prediction the directly given occurrences of the sense world, without introducing an artificial world picture.

First of all, it is easy to see that the reliability of a prediction depends, to a high degree, on the individual personality of the one who is making it. If we consider again weather forecasts, it makes a great difference whether tomorrow's weather is forecast by an amateur who knows nothing about today's atmospheric pressure, wind direction, atmospheric temperature and humidity, or by a capable farmer who considers all these data and also has a great deal of experience, or finally, by a scientifically trained metereologist who in addition to the local data also has access to the accurate information supplied by a great many

weather-maps from near and far. The forecast of
the experienced farmer is more reliable than that
of the amateur, and the forecast of the trained
metereologist more reliable than that of either of
those two. In view of this circumstance, it seems
natural to suppose that an ideal intellect, inti-
mately familiar with the most minute details of
physical processes occuring concurrently everywhere, would be able to predict tomorrow's
weather in all its details with an absolute accuracy. The same idea applies to every other prediction of physical occurrences.

Such an assumption signifies an extrapolation
which cannot be demonstrated logically, though
it cannot be refused in an *a priori* fashion either;
it must therefore be judged not on the score of its
truth, but only on the basis of its value. In consequence the actual impossibility of predicting even
a single occurrence accurately in classical as well
as in quantum physics, appears to be a natural
consequence of the circumstance that man with
his sense organs and measuring instruments is
himself a part of nature, subject to its laws and
confined within its limits, whereas the ideal intellect is free of all such limitations.

However, in order to be able to follow through such a view logically, we must comply with an important requirement: We must be on our guard against the temptation to make the ideal intellect the object of a scientific analysis, to regard it as something analogous to ourselves, and to ask of it how it obtains the knowledge which enables it to make precise predictions. The inquisitive human being who would do so, is quite likely to hear this answer to his question: "You resemble the intellect which you comprehend, not *me!*" And if after this reprimand he persists in his obstinacy and declares the concept of an ideal intellect to be meaningless and unnecessary, if not illogical, let him be reminded that not all statements which lack a logical foundation are scientifically worthless, and that his short-sighted formalism stops up the very fountain at which a Galileo, a Kepler, a Newton, and many other great physicists have quenched their thirst for scientific knowledge and insight. For all these men devotion to science was, consciously or unconsciously, a matter of faith— a matter of a serene faith in a rational world order.

Of course, this faith can no more be forced upon anybody than could one be commanded to see the truth or forbidden to commit an error. But the plain fact that we are able, at least to a certain degree, to subject future natural occurrences to our thought processes and to bend them to our will, would be a totally incomprehensible mystery, did it not permit us to surmise at least a certain harmony between the external world and the human intellect. The depth to which one conceives this harmony to extend is a matter of merely secondary importance.

In conclusion we may therefore say: The law of causality is neither true nor false. It is rather a heuristic principle, a signpost—and in my opinion, our most valuable signpost—to help us find our bearings in a bewildering maze of occurrences, and to show us the direction in which scientific research must advance in order to achieve fertile results. The law of causality, which immediately impresses the awakening soul of the child and plants the untiring question *"Why?"* into his mouth, remains a lifelong companion of the scientist and confronts him incessantly with new

problems. For science is not a contemplative re-
pose amidst knowledge already gained, but is in-
defatigable work and an ever progressive development.

Religion and Natural Science *

In former days, when a natural scientist had to address a general audience of laymen on a subject taken from his own special field of activity, in order to awaken a certain interest in the minds of his listeners, he would be forced to link his discourse to certain palpable experiences and views of daily life, in the fields of technology, metereology or biology, and to use these as his starting points to explain the methods applied by science in order to push forward from concrete individual problems to a knowledge of universal laws. Not so today. The exact methodology now employed by natural science has proved to be so extraordinarily productive in the course of centuries that natural-scientific research nowadays dares approach also problems intuitively less obvious than those lying within the fields just mentioned, and is able to tackle successfully also prob-

* A Lecture, delivered in May, 1937.

lems in psychology, in epistemology, indeed even in general attitudes toward life, thereby subjecting these problems to a treatment that is thorough from its own point of view. We may justly say that in these days no question, be it ever so abstract, can arise in our civilization without being related, in one way or another, to a problem that can be handled by the methods of natural science.

Accordingly, I will not appear to be too bold as a student of nature in discussing religious problems. This is a subject, the significance of which for our entire civilization is becoming progressively more manifest and which will undoubtedly be of a decisive importance for the question as to the fate that awaits us.

I

"Tell me—how do you stand to religion?"—If Goethe's *Faust* contains at all a simple phrase that captivates even a sophisticated listener and arouses a hidden tension within him, it must be this worried question of an innocent girl, in fear

for her newly-found happiness, to her lover whom she recognizes as a higher authority. For this very same question is the one which from time immemorial has innerly moved and worried countless human beings in search of peace of mind and knowledge at the same time.

But Faust, slightly embarrassed by this candid question, can think offhand only of this mildly defensive reply: *"I want to deprive nobody of his sentiments and his church."*

I could choose no better phrase to introduce our subject. I have not the slightest intention to loosen the foundation under the feet of those among you who have made peace with their conscience and have gained that firm foothold which is a prime requisite of one's conduct in life. To do so would be a reprehensible undertaking, unfair both to those who feel so secure in their religious faith that they do not permit a natural-scientific knowledge to influence it in any manner whatever, as well as to those who feel no need for any particular religious activity and are fully contented with an intuitive ethics. But these latter are likely to represent a small minority only. For the history of all eras and races teaches us only all too impressively that the candid faith which nothing can confuse, such as that which religion instills in its followers who are busy in active life, is the very fountainhead of the mightiest incentives to significant creative achievements, in the field of politics no less than in the realms of art and science.

This candid faith—and let us not delude ourselves about this—no longer exists today, even among the great masses of the nation, nor can it be revived any longer by considerations and measures oriented toward the past. For "to believe" means "to recognize as a truth," and the knowledge of nature, continually advancing on incontestably safe tracks, has made it utterly impossible for a person possessing some training in natural science to recognize as founded on truth the many reports of extraordinary occurrences contradicting the laws of nature, of miracles which are still commonly regarded as essential supports and confirmations of religious doctrines, and which formerly used to be accepted as facts pure and simple, without doubt or criticism.

Therefore, he who is in earnest about his faith

and cannot bear to see it conflict with his scientific learning, must decide in his conscience whether in all honesty, he may still consider himself a member of a religious community whose creed incorporates a belief in miracles.

For a while many could still find a certain temporary reassurance by trying to steer a middle course and limiting themselves to accepting as true a few miracles of especial importance. But such an attitude is untenable in the long run. The faith in miracles must yield ground, step by step, before the steady and firm advance of the forces of science, and its total defeat is indubitably a mere matter of time. The young generation of our own era, which in any case is sharply critical, toward traditional views, no longer permits itself to be bound innerly by doctrines which it regards as contradictory to the laws of nature. And the spiritually most gifted members of the young generation in particular, those destined to be the future leaders of their nation and who not seldom harbour a burning desire for religious satisfaction, are the ones most painfully hit by such incongruities. They are the ones who must suffer most heavily if they are sincere in seeking a compromise between their religious and their scientific beliefs.

Under these circumstances, it is no wonder that the atheist movement which calls religion an arbitrary delusion invented by power-hungry priests and which has nothing but words of derision for the pious faith in a supreme power above man, is eagerly taking advantage of the progress of scientific knowledge; allegedly in alliance with natural science, the movement continues to spread at an ever quickening pace its disruptive influence over all nations and classes of mankind. I need not go here into a more detailed discussion of the fact that the victory of atheism would not only destroy the most valuable treasures of our civilization, but—what is even worse —would annihilate the very hope for a better future.

Thus, Marguerite's question to the man to whom she gave her love and trust gains a most profound significance also for those who anxiously endeavor to find out whether the progress of natural sciences is actually bringing about a destruction of true religion.

If we study Faust's concise reply, spoken with

all care and tenderness of feeling, we find that we cannot give it here as our own, for a double reason: First, we must remember that this reply, both in form and content, is designed for the power of comprehension of a simple uneducated girl, and is therefore not meant to impress the intellect as well as the emotions and the imagination. But then—and this consideration is of a more decisive importance—we must bear in mind that these words are spoken by a Faust ruled by sensual desire, a confederate of Mephistopheles. I am sure that the redeemed Faust, whom we meet at the end of the second part, would give a somewhat different answer to Marguerite's question. But I do not presume to conjecture on the secrets which the poet chose to keep permanently as his own. I prefer to attempt to cast some light, from the perspective of one trained in the spirit of exact scientific research, on the question of whether and to what extent a truly religious attitude is compatible with the facts of knowledge gained through natural science—or to express it more concisely: Whether a person trained in natural science can be truly religious at the same time.

For this purpose, first of all let us discuss two special questions, quite separately from each other. The first one is: What demands does religion make on the beliefs of its followers, and what are the characteristics of a genuine religious attitude? The second question is: What is the nature of the laws natural science teaches us, and what truths does it regard as indubitable?

Once we shall have answered these two questions, we shall be in the position to decide whether and to what extent the demands of religion are compatible with those of natural science, and therefore, whether religion and natural science can exist side by side without clashing with each other.

II

Religion is the link that binds man to his God. It is founded on a respectful humility before a super-natural power, to which all human life is subject, and which controls our weal and woe. To be in harmony with this power and to enjoy its good graces, is the incessant endeavor and supreme goal of the religious person. Only in this way can he feel protected from the foreseen and unforeseen dangers, which threaten him in this earthly life, and can he enjoy that purest of all happiness, the inner peace of mind and soul that is secured only by a firm link to God and by an unconditionally trusting faith in His omnipotence and benevolence. In this sense, religion is rooted in the consciousness of the individual.

But its significance transcends the individual. Instead of each individual possessing his own distinctive religion, religion seeks to become valid and meaningful for a larger community, for a nation, for a race, and ultimately for all of mankind. For God is the sovereign of every country on this earth; the whole world with all its treasures and all its horrors is subject to Him, and there is no portion either of the realm of nature or of the mind without His omnipresence.

Therefore, the spirit of religion unites its adherents in a universal alliance, and sets before them the task of mutually acquainting each other with their articles of faith and giving them a common manifestation. But this can be accomplished only by clothing the substance of religion in a definite external form, suitable because of its intuitive clarity for the creation of a mutual under-standing. In view of the great diversity of the races of man and of their ways of life, it is only natural that this external form is quite different in different parts of the world, so that a large variety of religions have come into existence in the course of the ages. A common feature of all of them consists in the rather natural assumption of a personified or at least an anthropomorphic deity. This leaves room for the most diverse con-cepts of the attributes of God. Each religion has its own distinct mythology and also its own dis-tinct rituals, elaborate to the most minute details in the more highly developed religions. These are the source of certain interpretive symbols of re-ligious worship, which are capable of acting di-rectly on the imagination of the great masses, arousing their interest in religious matters and giving them a certain understanding of the deity.

Thus, a systematic unification of mythological traditions and a strict observance of solemn ritual-istic customs invest the worship of God with an external symbolical form, and centuries of inces-sant observance and systematic education of gen-eration after generation increase the significance

of such religious symbols. The holiness of an un-
fathomable deity is translated into the holiness
of intelligible symbols. They are a source of
strong stimulation for the arts as well. In fact, the
mightiest benefits ever enjoyed by art were the
result of its becoming a servant to religion.

Yet, a careful distinction must be made here between art and religion. A work of art carries its
significance essentially within itself. Even though,
as a rule, it owes its origin to external circumstances and in consequence often awakens trains
of thought moving at a tangent, still it is basically
self-sufficient and requires no specific interpretation in order to be appreciated. This fact becomes
most clearly evident in music, most abstract of
all arts.

On the other hand, a religious symbol always
points beyond itself. Its significance is never ex-
hausted by its own features, however much veneration it may enjoy because of its own age and
the operation of a pious tradition. It is important to emphasize this because the development of
civilization makes the high esteem enjoyed by certain religious symbols subject to certain inevitable changes in the course of the centuries, and it

is in the interest of a genuine spirit of religion to establish the fact that what stands behind and above these symbols is unaffected by such changes.

To cite here just one of a great many specific examples: A winged angel has been regarded from time immemorial as the most beautiful symbol for a servant and messenger of God. But there can be found among persons trained in anatomy, some whose scientifically conditioned imagination does not permit them, despite their best intentions, to see any beauty in such a physiological impossibility. Nevertheless, this circumstance need have not the slightest adverse effect on their religious convictions. They ought, however, to be on their guard not to impair or destroy the pious attitudes of those who still find solace and edification in the sight of a winged angel.

But the overrating of the significance of religious symbols opens the gates to another, far more serious danger of an onslaught by the atheistic movement. It is one of the favorite techniques of the atheists, whose aim is the undermining of every true religious feeling, to direct their attacks against old-established religious rites and customs and to hold them up to ridicule or contempt as outmoded anachronisms. Through such attacks against symbols, they expect to hurt religion itself, and the more strange and conspicuous those views and customs are, the easier it is for the atheists to score a success. Many a religious soul has succumbed to these tactics.

Against this peril there is no better defense than to understand clearly and thoroughly that a religious symbol, be it ever so venerable, never represents an absolute value but is always only a more or less imperfect sign of something higher and not directly accessible to human senses.

Under these circumstances, it is quite understandable that the history of religions records the frequent recurrence of the idea to restrict or even eliminate completely the use of religious symbols and to treat religion more as a matter of abstract reasoning. But even a brief reflection shows such an idea to be entirely inadequate. Without symbols, human beings could not communicate with each other at all. This applies not only to religious communication, but to all human transactions in secular daily life as well. Language itself is actually nothing else than a symbol for something higher—for thought. To be sure, individual words also arouse a typical interest in themselves, but viewed more closely, a word is just a series of letters; its meaning lies fundamentally in the concept which it expresses. And it is basically of a secondary importance whether the concept is represented by one word rather than by another, in one particular language rather than another. If the word is translated into another language, the concept itself remains unaffected.

Another example: A flag is the symbol of the glory and honor of a regiment of soldiers. The older the flag, the higher its value. In the heat of the battle, the bearer of the flag considers it to be his supreme duty not to desert the honored emblem at any cost, to protect it with his own body if need be, even to give his life for it if he must. Yet, a flag is just a symbol, a piece of a bright-colored cloth. The enemy can capture it, soil, mutilate it, but can never destroy the higher concept, of which it is the symbol. The regiment will still retain its honor, get a new flag, and perhaps exact suitable retribution for the insult to its emblem.

Just as in an army—and more generally in every community of men facing great tasks together—religion also finds symbols and their corresponding ecclesiastical rituals absolutely indispensable. They signify the highest and most venerated of all the products of human imagination directed heavenward. But we must never forget that even the most sacred symbol is of human origin.

Had mankind taken this truth to heart at all times, it would have been spared an infinity of woe and suffering. For the terrible religious wars, the horrible persecutions of heretics and their attendant tragic consequences, are in the last analysis the outcome of conflicts between opposing propositions, each possessing a certain validity and each originating in the circumstances that a common abstract idea, such as the belief in an omnipotent God, was confused with its visible but distinct media of expression, such as ecclesiastic articles of faith. Certainly there is nothing more distressing than the bitter fight of two adversaries, each of whom is fully convinced of the rightness of his cause and is filled with honest enthusiasm for it, feeling that he must devote all his energy to the battle, even sacrifice his life in it. How much productive work could have been accomplished if in the domain of religious activity such valuable energies had been united instead of employed for mutual extermination.

The deeply religious individual who gives expression to his belief in God through a veneration of his beloved sacred symbols, does not insist on them blindly, but has an understanding for the fact that there can be other persons as deeply religious as himself to whom other symbols are no less beloved and sacred,—just as a definite concept remains unaltered whether it is expressed by one word or another, in one language or another.

But a comprehension of this state of affairs still does not explain the nature of the characteristic features of true religious conviction. For now another question, the one of the truly fundamental significance, must be answered: Does that higher power which stands behind the religious symbols and lends them their essential significance, dwell solely in the human mind, and is it obliterated also in the moment when that mind ceases to exist, or does it stand for something more? In

other words: Does God live in the soul of the believer only, or does He rule the world independently of whether or not one believes in Him? This
is the point at which minds part company basically and decisively. This question can never be
cleared up scientifically, by logical conclusions
based on facts. The answer is solely and exclusively a matter of faith—religious faith.

The answer of the religious person is that God
exists, that He existed before there were human
beings on the earth, that he holds the whole
world, believers as well as disbelievers, in His
omnipotent hands since the beginning of eternity,
and that He will continue to rule from His
heights inaccessible to human imagination long
after the earth and everything on it will have
crumbled to dust. All those who profess this belief and, filled by it with humility and unques-
tioning trust and devotion, feel protected by the
Almighty from every danger in life, all those—
but only those—may consider themselves truly
religious.

This is the essential content of creed which religion requires its followers to profess. Let us

now see whether and how these requirements are compatible with those of science, natural science in particular.

III

In proceeding to examine what laws science teaches us, and what truths it considers to be inviolable, our task will be simplified and our purpose fully served by keeping to the most exact of all natural sciences, physics. For this is the branch of science which by every logic could be expected to be the most likely to conflict with the demands of religion. Therefore, we are to inquire what kind of discoveries physical science has made up to our most recent days, and what limits these might set for religious faith.

I hardly need to point out that viewed historically and on the whole, the findings of physical research and the conclusions resulting from them do not exhibit a purposeless change, but have been steadily improving in precision and completeness until the most recent days, some times at a faster at other times at a slower rate; and we therefore have every reason to regard the knowledge thus far accumulated by physical science as being of a lasting character.

What then is the substance of these findings? First of all, it must be noted that all data of physical knowledge are founded on measurements, and that every measurement takes place in space and time with the orders of magnitudes varying from the inconceivably vast to the infinitesimally small. We can get an approximate idea of the distance of the cosmic regions from which a message can still reach us if we consider that light, which traverses the distance from the Moon to the Earth in a second or so, requires many millions of years to arrive from those regions to our planet. On the other side of the picture, physical science must calculate with spatial and temporal magnitudes, the infinite smallness of which can be realized by the comparison of a head of a pin with our entire planet.

Measurements of the most varied kinds have been consistent in leading to the conclusions that all physical occurrences without exception can be reduced to mechanical or electrical processes, produced by the movements of certain elementary particles, such as electrons, positrons, protons and neutrons; and both the mass and the charge of all of these particles are each expressed by an extremely small but quite definite number. The precision of this number increases with improvements in the accuracy of methods of measurement. These minute numbers, the so-called universal constants, are in a sense the immutable building blocks of the edifice of theoretic physics.

So now we must continue with the question: What is the real meaning of these constants? Are they, in the last analysis, inventions of the inquiring mind of man, or do they possess a real meaning independent of human intelligence?

The first of these two views is professed by the followers of Positivism, or at least by its most extreme partisans. Their theory is that physical science has no other foundation than the measurements on which its structure is erected, and that a proposition in physics makes any sense only insofar as it can be supported by measurements. But since every measurement presupposes an observer, from the positivistic viewpoint the real substance of a law of physics can never be detached from the observer, and it loses its meaning as soon as one attempts mentally to eliminate the observer and to see something more, something real, behind him and his measurement.

This outlook cannot be challenged from the purely logical viewpoint. And yet, a closer examination must brand this version of it as inadequate and unproductive. For it disregards a circumstance which is of a decisive importance in the extension and progress of scientific knowledge. However much Positivism may regard itself as proceeding without presuppositions, it is nonetheless committed to a fundamental premise if it is not to degenerate into an unintelligible solipsism. This premise is that every physical measurement can be reproduced, so that its outcome depends neither on the personality of the individual performing the experiment, nor on the place and time of the measurement, nor on any other attendant circumstance. But this simply means that the factor which is decisive for the result of the measurement lies beyond the observer, and that one is therefore necessarily led to questions concerning real causal connections operating independently of the observer.

To be sure, it must be agreed that the positivistic outlook possesses a distinctive value; for it is instrumental to a conceptual clarification of the significance of physical laws, to a separation of that which is empirically proven from that which is not, to an elimination of emotional prejudices nurtured solely by customary views, and it thus helps to clear the road for the onward drive of research. But Positivism lacks the driving force for serving as a leader on this road. True, it is able to eliminate obstacles, but it cannot turn them into productive factors. For its activity is essentially critical, its glance is directed backward. But progress, advancement requires new associations of ideas and new queries, not based on the results of measurements alone, but going beyond them, and toward such things the fundamental attitude of Positivism is one of aloofness.

Therefore, up to quite recently, positivists of all hues have also put up the strongest resistance to the introduction of atomic hypotheses and thereby also to the acceptance of the above mentioned universal constants. This is quite understandable, for the existence of these constants is a palpable proof of the existence in nature of something real and independent of every human measurement.

Of course, even to-day a consistent positivist could call the universal constants mere inventions which have proved to be uncommonly useful in making possible an accurate and complete description of the most diversified results of measurements. But hardly any real physicist would take such an assertion seriously. The universal constants were not invented for reasons of practical convenience, but have forced themselves upon us irresistibly because of the agreement between the results of all relevant measurements, and— this is the essential thing—we know quite well in advance that all future measurements will lead to these selfsame constants.

To sum it all up, we can say that physical science demands that we admit the existence of a real world independent from us, a world which we can however never recognize directly but can apprehend only through the medium of our sense experiences and of the measurements mediated by them.

If we pursue this principle further, our outlook on the world takes a different form. The subject of the observation, the observing Ego, loses its position at the focus of thought and is relegated to a quite modest place. In fact, how pitifully small, how powerless we human beings must appear to ourselves if we stop to think that the planet Earth on which we live our lives is just a minute, infinitesimal mote of dust; on the other hand how peculiar it must seem that we, tiny creatures on a tiny planet, are nevertheless capable of knowing though not the essence at least the existence and the dimensions of the basic building blocks of the entire great Cosmos!

But this is still not the end of the wonder of it. Physical research has established as an incontestable fact that these basic building blocks of the Universe do not exist unrelated in isolated groups, but that all of them are mutually interlinked according to one uniform plan. In other words, every process in nature is subject to a universal and up to a point knowable law.

I want to mention at this place just one example: The law of the conservation of energy. There are various forms of energy in nature—kinetic energy, the energy of gravity, heat, electricity, magnetism. All the energies together form the energy supply of the world. The quantity of this energy supply is constant; it cannot be increased or diminished by any process in nature. All changes in nature are in reality simply the transformations of one form of energy into another. For instance, when kinetic energy is lost by friction, an equivalent quantity of thermal energy results.

The law of the conservation of energy is valid in every branch and field of physics, both according to the classical theory and to quantum mechanics. To be sure, there have often been attempts to challenge its precise validity in connection with the processes taking place within a single atom, and to assign to it a mere statistical significance for such processes. But every single experiment thus far undertaken has shown that such attempts are futile, and there is no reason to deny that the law of the conservation of energy is an absolutely and universally valid law of nature.

Those with positivistic leanings counter frequently with the critical objection that there is nothing extraordinary about the universal validity of such a law. According to them the explanation of the mystery is simply that after all it is man himself who prescribes the laws for nature. And in claiming this, they even cite Immanuel Kant in support of this view.

However, as I have pointed it out, the laws of nature were not invented by man, but external factors forced him to recognize them. An *a priori* approach to the laws of nature, as well as to the universal constants, could make us imagine them quite differently from what they are in reality. But the positivist reference to Kant is based on a gross misunderstanding. Kant did not teach that man actually prescribes laws for nature. He taught simply that whenever man formulates the laws of nature, he always adds something of his own, too. Otherwise how would it be conceivable that according to Kant's own statement, no external impression inspired in him a more profound feeling of respectful humility than the sight of the starry skies? After all, respectful humility is not exactly the attitude which a man is in the habit of assuming toward a rule formulated by himself. Obviously, such sentiment is alien to the mind of a positivist. To him the stars are nothing more than complexes of optical sensations; he considers everything else as just a useful but basically arbitrary and unessential trimming.

But let us now leave Positivism and continue with our own train of thought. The law of the conservation of energy is, after all, not the only law of nature, it is just one among many. While it is true that it is universally valid, it is still not sufficient for predicting every detail of a natural process, since it leaves an endless number of possibilities still open.

But there is another, far broader law, which has the property of giving a specific, unequivocal answer to each and every sensible question concerning the course of a natural process; as far as we can see, this law—like the law of the conservation of energy—possesses an exact validity even for the most modern parts of physics. But what we must regard as the greatest wonder of all, is the fact that the most adequate formulation of this law creates the impression in every unbiased mind that nature is ruled by a rational, purposive will.

Let me illustrate this by a specific example. It is a well known fact that when a ray of light strikes the surface of a transparent body obliquely, such as the surface of water, it is deflected from its original direction after penetrating the surface. The explanation of this deflection is that light travels more slowly in water than in air. Such deflection, or "refraction," occurs also in the atmosphere, because light travels more slowly in the lower, denser strata of the asmosphere than in its higher layers. Now then, when a light ray emitted by a star reaches the eyes of an observer, its path will show a more or less complicated curve, due to the different degrees of refraction in the various atmospheric layers (unless the star happens to be exactly in the zenith). This curve is fully determined by the following simple law: Out of all the possible paths leading from the star to the eye of the observer, light will always follow the one which it can cover in the shortest time, allowance being made for the differences in its velocity in different atmospheric layers. Thus, the photons which constitute a ray of light behave like intelligent beings: Out of all the possible curves they always select the one which will take them most quickly to their goal.

This principle permits a large-scale generalization. According to all that we know about the laws relating to the processes taking place in any physical structure, we can characterize in all its details the course of each process by the principle that among all the conceivable processes which can change the state of a given physical structure into another state during a certain time interval, the process which actually takes place is always one for which the integral over that time interval of a certain magnitude, the so-called Lagrange function, has the smallest value. Therefore, if we know the value of the Lagrange function, we can fully specify the course of the process actually taking place.

It is certainly no wonder that the discovery of this law—the so-called least-action principle, after which the elementary quantum of action was later also named,—made its discoverer Leibniz, and soon after him also his follower Maupertuis, so boundlessly enthusiastic; for these scientists believed themselves to have found in it a tangible evidence for a ubiquitous higher reason ruling all nature.

In fact, the least-action principle introduces a completely new idea into the concept of causality: The *causa efficiens*, which operates from the present into the future and makes future situations appear as determined by earlier ones, is joined by

the *causa finalis* for which, inversely, the future—
namely, a definite goal—serves as the premise
from which there can be deduced the development
of the processes which lead to this goal.

So long as we confine ourselves to the realm of
physics, these alternative points of view are
merely different mathematical expressions for one
and the same fact, and it would be futile to ask
which of the two came nearer to the truth. The
choice between them depends solely on practical
considerations. The chief advantage of the least-
action principle is that it requires no definite
frame of reference for its formulation. This principle is therefore excellently adapted for carrying
through transformation of coordinates.

But we are now interested in questions of a
more general character. It will suffice at this point
to note only that the historical development of
theoretic research in physics has led in a remarkable way to a formulation of the principle of
physical causality which possesses an explicitly
teleological character; but at the same time this
formulation introduces nothing substantially new
or even contradictory into the character of the
laws of nature. The issue is simply one of different

perspectives of interpretation, both of which are equally well justified by the actual facts. The situation in biology should be no different than we have found it in physics, although in biology the difference between the two viewpoints has assumed far sharper outlines.

In any case, we may say in summary that according to what exact natural science teaches us, the entire realm of nature, in which we human beings on our tiny mote of a planet play only an infinitesimally small part, is ruled by definite laws which are independent of the existence of thinking human beings; but these laws, insofar as they can at all be comprehended by our senses, can be given a formulation which is adapted for purposeful activity. Thus, natural science exhibits a rational world order to which nature and mankind are subject, but a world order the inner essence of which is and remains unknowable to us, since only our sense data (which can never be completely excluded) supply evidence for it. Nevertheless, the truly prolific results of natural-scientific research justify the conclusion that continuing efforts will at least keep bringing us progressively nearer to the inattainable goal, and they strengthen our inner hope for a constant advancement of our insight into the ways of the omnipotent Reason which rules over Nature.

IV

Having now learned to know the demands which religion on one hand and science on the other hand place on our attitude to the most sublime problems of a generalized world outlook, let us now examine whether and to what extent these different demands can be mutually reconciled. First of all, it is self-evident that this examination may extend only to those laws in which religion and natural science conflict with each other. For these are wide spheres where they have absolutely nothing to do with each other. Thus, all the problems of ethics are outside of the field of natural science, whereas the dimensions of the universal constants are without relevance for religion.

On the other hand, religion and natural science do have a point of contact in the issue concerning the existence and nature of a supreme power ruling the world, and here the answers given by them are to a certain degree at least comparable.

As we have seen, they are by no means mutually contradictory, but are in agreement, first of all, on the point that there exists a rational world order independent from man, and secondly, on the view that the character of this world order can never be directly known but can only be indirectly recognized or suspected. Religion employs in this connection its own characteristic symbols, while natural science uses measurements founded on sense experiences. Thus nothing stands in our way——and our instinctive intellectual striving for a unified world picture demands it——from identifying with each other the two everywhere active and yet mysterious forces: The world order of natural science and the God of religion. Accordingly, the deity which the religious person seeks to bring closer to himself by his palpable symbols, is consubstantial with the power acting in accordance with natural laws for which the sense data of the scientist provide a certain degree of evidence.

However, in spite of this unanimity a fundamental difference must also be observed. To the religious person, God is directly and immediately given. He and His omnipotent Will are the fountainhead of all life and all happenings, both in the mundane world and in the world of the spirit. Even though He cannot be grasped by reason, the religious symbols give a direct view of Him, and He plants His holy message in the souls of those who faithfully entrust themselves to Him. In contrast to this, the natural scientist recognizes as immediately given nothing but the content of his sense experiences and of the measurements based on them. He starts out from this point, on a road of inductive research, to approach as best he can the supreme and eternally unattainable goal of his quest—God and His world order. Therefore, while both religion and natural science require a belief in God for their activities, to the former He is the starting point, to the latter the goal of every thought process. To the former He is the foundation, to the latter the crown of the edifice of every generalized world view.

This difference corresponds to the different roles of religion and natural science in human life. Natural science wants man to learn, religion wants him to act. The only solid foundation for learning is the one supplied by sense perception; the assumption of a regular world order functions here merely as an essential condition for formulating fruitful questions. But this is not the road to be taken for action, for man's volitional decisions cannot wait until cognition has become complete or he has become omniscient. We stand in the midst of life, and its manifold demands and needs often make it imperative that we reach decisions or translate our mental attitudes into immediate action. Long and tedious reflection cannot enable us to shape our decisions and attitudes properly; only that definite and clear instruction can which we gain from a direct inner link to God. This instruction alone is able to give us the inner firmness and lasting peace of mind which must be regarded as the highest boon in life. And if we ascribe to God, in addition to His omnipotence and omniscience, also the attributes of goodness and love, recourse to Him produces an increased feeling of safety and happiness in the human being thirsting for solace. Against this conception not even the slightest objection can be raised from the point of view of natural science, for as we pointed it out before, questions of ethics are entirely outside of its realm.

No matter where and how far we look, nowhere

do we find a contradiction between religion and natural science. On the contrary, we find a complete concordance in the very points of decisive importance. Religion and natural science do not exclude each other, as many contemporaries of ours would believe or fear; they mutually supplement and condition each other. The most immediate proof of the compatibility of religion and natural science, even under the most thorough critical scrutiny, is the historic fact that the very greatest natural scientists of all times—men such as Kepler, Newton, Leibniz—were permeated by a most profound religious attitude. At the dawn of our own era of civilization, the practitioners of natural science were the custodians of religion at the same time. The oldest of all the applied natural sciences, medicine, was in the hands of the priests, and in the Middle Ages scientific research was still carried on principally in monasteries. Later, as civilization continued to advance and to branch out, the parting of the ways became always more pronounced, corresponding to the different nature of the tasks and pursuits of religion and those of natural science.

For the proper attitude to questions in ethics

can no more be gained from a purely rational cognition than can a general *Weltanschauung* ever replace specific knowledge and ability. But the two roads do not diverge; they run parallel to each other, and they intersect at an endlessly removed common goal.

There is no better way to comprehend this properly than to continue one's efforts to obtain a progressively more profound insight into the nature and problems of the natural sciences, on one hand, and of religious faith on the other. It will then appear with ever increasing clarity that even though the methods are different—for science operates predominantly with the intellect, religion predominantly with sentiment—the significance of the work and the direction of progress are nonetheless absolutely identical.

Religion and natural science are fighting a joint battle in an incessant, never relaxing crusade against scepticism and against dogmatism, against disbelief and against superstition, and the rallying cry in this crusade has always been, and always will be: *"On to God!"*

Index

INDEX

INDEX

Kant, Immanuel, 176
Karsten, Gustav, 21
Kassel, 8
Kepler, 148, 186
Kiel, 7
kinetic theory of gases, 37, 42
Kirchhoff, Gustav, 9, 15, 19, 24, 111
Kirchhoff's Law, 34
knowledge, 69, 86
Koch, Robert, 114
Kurlbaum, F., 39

L, see Laschmidt number
Lagrange function, 179
language, as symbols, 162-163
law
  of causality, 121, 138ff, 149
  experimental, 55
  statistical, 126
  of thermodynamics, 16, 17, 23, 29
least-action, principle of, 48, 179-180
Lehmann-Filhés, Rudolf, 15
Leibniz, 44, 179, 186
Leipzig, 19
light, 56
  electromagnetic theory of, 35
  emission theory, 59
  velocity of, 47, 97, 98
  wave theory of, 59
logic, 82, 88
Loschmidt, J., 42
Loschmidt number, 43
luminiferous ether, 56
Lummer, O., 34, 39, 41

Mach, Ernst, 30
Manpertius, 179
Marguerite, 157
mass, 99
mathematical symbols, 128
mathematics
  abstract, 110
  laws of, 82
matrices, Heisenberg's, 136
matter, particulate nature of, 59
  wave nature of, 59
Maximilian-Gymnasium, 13, 14
Maxwell, Clerke, 35
measure, measurement, 81, 101, 110,
  173, 183
  accuracy in, 104-110, 169-170
  effect of instruments in, 142-143
  interpretation of physical, 142-143
mechanics, 99, 135
mental forces, 62
mental state, 65, 66
Mephistopheles, 157
metaphysical world, 101
  reality, 102
meteorology, 123
method
  experimental, 107
  of observation, influence of, 70

method—*Continued*
  of investigation, 139
  scientific, 45
  theoretical, 107
methodology, of the natural sciences,
  151
Michelson and Morely experiment,
  139
Middle Ages, 186
mind problem, 60ff
mind, subconscious, 66
miracles, belief in, 154-155
molecular disorder, assumption of,
  33, 37
molecular velocity, 126
molecules, 132
moles, see gram-molecules
momentum, 133
  of a point, 134, 135
Mommsen, Theodor, 82
Monism, 81
Monists, 81
Morley, see Michelson
motion, molecular, 125-127
  see also Brownian movement
Müller, Hermann, 13, 14
Munich, 13, 14, 20, 25
  University of, 14
music, 161
mythology, 160

Nagasaki, 117
natural laws, 93
natural science, 112, 156-157, 168
  and religion, 151ff
Nernst, W., 27, 48
Neumann, Carl, 19
neutron, 115
Newton, Sir Isaac, 44, 59, 148, 186
Normal Spectral Energy Distribution, 34
nuclear energy, 116
nuclear physics, 55, 112
nuclear reactions, 115
nuclei, atomic, of uranium, 115

objects, physical, 94-95
observation, influence of, 70-71
  external and internal view points,
  72
*On the Principle of The Increase of
  Entropy,* 23
operators, Schrödinger's, 136
optics, 124
oscillations, mean energy of, 132
oscillators, linear, 35-36, 37
osmotic pressure, 28
Ostwald, Wilhelm, 28, 30, 32

Paalzow, Adolph, 25
pain, sensation of, 66-67
particle, 59
pencils of light, 43

INDEX

INDEX

CPSIA information can be obtained at www.ICGtesting.com
Printed in the USA
LVOW07s0139220616

493523LV00001B/150/P